TT507 .F583 2008

Fletcher, Kate,

Sustainable fashion and
 textiles design journeys
      2008.

2009 01 27

W9-DAX-619
0 1341 1156182 2

Sustainable Fashion and Textiles

Design Journeys

HUMBER COLLEGE
LAKESHORE CAMPUS
LEARNING RESOURCE CENTRE
3199 LAKESHORE BLVD. WEST
TORONTO, ONTARIO M8V 1K8

For Mark, Jude and Cole

165101

Sustainable Fashion and Textiles

Design Journeys

Kate Fletcher

London • Sterling, VA

First published by Earthscan in the UK and USA in 2008
Reprinted 2008

Copyright © Kate Fletcher, 2008

All rights reserved

ISBN-13: 978-1-84407-463-1 Hardback
ISBN-13: 978-1-84407-481-5 Paperback
Typeset by Safehouse Creative
Printed and bound by Gutenberg Press, Malta
Cover design by Lucy Jane Batchelor

For a full list of publications please contact:

Earthscan
Dunstan House, 14a St Cross Street
London, EC1N 8XA, UK
Tel: +44 (0)20 7841 1930
Fax: +44 (0)20 7242 1474
Email: earthinfo@earthscan.co.uk
Web: www.earthscan.co.uk

22883 Quicksilver Drive, Sterling, VA 20166-2012, USA

Earthscan publishes in association with the International Institute for Environment
and Development

A catalogue record for this book is available from the British Library

Library of Congress Cataloging-in-Publication Data
Fletcher, Kate, 1971-
    Sustainable fashion and textiles design journeys / Kate Fletcher.
        p. cm.
    Includes bibliographical references and index.
    ISBN 978-1-84407-463-1 (hardback) – ISBN 978-1-84407-481-5 (pbk.)
 1. Fashion design. 2. Textile design. 3. Sustainable design. I. Title.

TT507.F583 2008
746.9'2–dc22

2007041580

The paper used for this book is FSC-certified and elemental chlorine-free.

Mixed Sources
Product group from well-managed
forests, and other controlled sources
www.fsc.org Cert no. TT-CoC-002424
© 1996 Forest Stewardship Council
FSC

Contents

List of Figures, Tables and Images

Figures

Tables

Images

Acknowledgements

I thank Lynda Grose, one of my first readers, whose advice, wisdom and encouragement continues to keep me going. My gratitude to Lucy Batchelor whose support, friendship and gorgeous design work has made such a difference and has been so gratefully received. Thank you to Toni Spencer and Arran Derbyshire for reading sections of the book, along with the many others who gave feedback and advice when it was so badly needed. Thank you also to Mathilda Tham, Anna Harvey, William Lana, Damien Sanfillippo, Lee Holdstock, Ann Thorpe and Otto von Busch for so freely sharing their ideas and information with me. I would like to thank all of those who provided images for this book and who work so creatively and passionately to promote sustainability in the fashion and textile sector. I thank all the people with whom I've cut my design for sustainability teeth over the years, particularly Emma Dewberry. Thank you to Tamsine O'Riordan, Camille Adamson and Dan Harding at Earthscan who have treated me so well and have worked hard to get this book out.

Most of all I thank my husband, whose scientific brain I borrow to clarify ideas, whose love of short sentences has helped pare down the curlicues of my writing style and who has looked after our two big small boys on his own a lot over the last six months just to give me room to think.

Introduction

This book explores sustainability issues in fashion and textiles. It does this from the perspective of design. Here design is used in its broadest sense, not just as a stylist or shaper of things (though this too has an important role), but also as a promoter of social change. Thus, while this book is about design, it is not just for designers. It is relevant to anyone who is interested in taking action and cultivating change towards sustainability. *Sustainable Fashion and Textiles: Design Journeys* explores this action and change through the complex, creative and consumerism-dominated world of fashion and textiles.

The aim of this book is to promote a broad, pluralistic view of sustainability ideas, issues and opportunities in the fashion and textile sector. The goal is to show that there is a wealth of different ways in which we can go about building long-lasting environmental and social quality through the design, production and use of fashion and textiles that go beyond traditional ideas or expectations. After all, the challenge of sustainability – that is, of integrating human well-being and natural integrity – is such that we can't go on as before. Business as usual or, more to the point, fashion as usual, is not an option. So what should we do instead? The answer, described in the pages that follow, can be found in embracing a multiplicity of starting points, involving many different people, operating across a range of different time scales. The effect is to produce an array of more diverse, engaging and resourceful fashion and textiles that secures employment for millions of workers, gives manufacturing industry an opportunity to trial and develop cutting-edge technologies and approaches that dramatically reduce resource use, and uses the catalytic potential of design to bring change.

This book offers eight different starting points or 'design journeys' from which we can begin to explore these opportunities. Each journey is explored in a separate chapter and covers different, though interrelated, sustainability ground. The journeys described in this book evoke a sense of a landscape. As an analogy, the world of sustainable textiles and fashion is a place of mountains, valleys, plateaus and swampy ground. The mountains rise up like beacons or navigation points and show us ideals, values and direction (where do we want to head?). The valleys in between represent where we are now – at the beginnings of our journey, in the rich, fertile and enthusiastic soil of ideas and possibilities, and still perhaps a little unsure of how the landscape will unfold. The swamps and plateaus represent the difficult terrain where progress is slow. Perhaps it is uncharted territory, a dead end or the start of a potentially exciting new area of investigation. Yet no matter how bogged down we become or whichever vantage point we climb to, we have a sense that no part of this world exists in isolation from the rest. The landscape is a whole and it unfolds before us, changing, eroding and rising up over time.

The design journeys in this book begin in Chapter 1 by navigating the complexities of sustainability impacts of materials, and conclude in Chapter 8 with a voyage into participatory design and open-source initiatives relevant to fashion and textiles. None of them deals with entirely new or futuristic ideas. All of them, or at least almost all of them, already exist to a greater or lesser extent in the fashion and textile sector today. This book draws them together into a holistic, multilayered and more sustainable vision for the sector. This is a radical vision, but not an extreme one. Such a vision, in the words of industrial ecologist John Ehrenfeld, 'brings us back to our roots – the meaning at the very origin of "radical" – and is the natural way to go'.[1] This roots-based, nature-inspired and interconnected vision is developed throughout the book.

There are commonly thought to be two different value systems or world-views that influence the approach we take to sustainability.[2] Crudely simplifying things, the first can be described as 'more of the same, but more efficient' and involves making incremental changes to our present-day institutions and practices to bring about improvements. The second sees sustainability as necessitating 'something different'. That is, something different to greater efficiency, also involving fundamental personal, social and institutional change. This book is a blend of these two views. It is structured around ideas from the 'something different' paradigm but infuses this structure with many of the pragmatic, resourceful techniques and experience that have been developed from incremental change in today's fashion and textile sector. The result is a collection of long-term and short-term solutions that help us ground our work in inter-generational sustainability values and yet still be able to make decisions today that are simple, practical and insightful.

Sustainable Fashion and Textiles: Design Journeys is thus part handbook, part vision. It brings together information about lifecycle sustainability impacts of fashion and textiles, practical alternatives, ecological concepts and social innovation. The book defines the key relationships between sustainability and the fashion and textile sector and it also challenges the sector to change. Arranged in two parts, the first four chapters of this book represent key phases of the textile product lifecycle. Chapter 1 explores the impacts of cultivating or extracting textile fibres; Chapter 2 focuses on the production phase of the lifecycle; Chapter 3, the use phase; and Chapter 4, issues associated with end of life. Each of these chapters explores opportunities to improve the sustainability of that lifecycle phase supported by data and case studies, and reframes the issues in a holistic context. The remaining four chapters focus on the sustainability of fashion and textiles at the systems level, and explore opportunities to influence the root cause of many sustainability problems. Chapter 5 considers the relationship between fashion and consumption and reviews the ideas of designing for fundamental human needs. Chapter 6 explores the possibility of developing local products and those that are more resource efficient (i.e. light). Chapter 7 investigates issues associated with speed and in particular describes slow fashion. And finally Chapter 8 surveys participatory design and examines its potential for promoting sustainability.

While each of the chapters in this book is complete in and of itself, they are not autonomous or separate from each other. The first four lifecycle-focused chapters clearly relate to each other in a dynamic way, and the final four seek to influence the overall system of which the first four are a part. Thus the chapters' real value comes from what they represent together: innovative ways of thinking about fabrics and garments based on sustainability values and a broad, interconnected view of design. This broad view of design has been described by the scientist Herb Simon: 'Everyone designs who devises courses of action aimed at changing existing situations into preferred ones'.[3] So in the context of this book, any actions or ideas that help facilitate change towards sustainability are embraced as design. This is a broad category and includes the work of community groups, big companies and individual con-sumers, as well as professional designers. What the authors of these actions and ideas have in common is that they are using practical skills and creative thinking to innovate (normally with a group of other people) to produce prod-ucts, ways of working or visions compatible with sustainability. Giving form to sustainability in any or all of these ways is vital if it is to become a reality. As the Nobel prize-winning economist Amartya Sen said 'it is difficult to desire what one cannot imagine as a possibility'. The hope is that this book can help us both desire and imagine sustainability better.

▲ The sustainability landscape

PART ONE Sustainable Fashion and Textile Products

CHAPTER ONE Material Diversity

Materials play an emphatic role in our current understanding of what makes fashion and textiles sustainable. They are, more often than not, our starting point for change and a key commodity for farmer, designer, manufacturing industry, consumer and recycler. Indeed materials have been at the centre of both recent waves of interest in sustainable fashion and textiles. In the first, in the early 1990s, natural and recycled fibres dominated trade shows, trend predictions and industry journals. In the second, in the mid part of the 2000s, organic, Fair Trade and rapidly renewable fibres have led design innovation, with many companies basing their collections on choice of 'alternative' materials. The fact that materials seem to dominate our ideas about environmental and social responsibility is not really surprising as, after all, our industry's product is material 'stuff' – fibre, fabric, textile product and garment. For all of these reasons this chapter is the first in this book. Its aim is to quench the thirst for information about resource consumption, energy use, pollution potential and social impact of textile fibres, providing an information-rich resource that can support our design choices. But this chapter also has a broader and deeper goal, to frame knowledge about fibres in a way that promotes a change in perspective, and to challenge us to think beyond materials and to link a fibre with its lifecycle, a material with a user, and an industry with the ecological and cultural systems that support it.

In this chapter (as the title suggests), the sustainability impacts of produ-cing textile fibres are linked to the ecosystem-inspired idea of diversity. The fusion of fashion and textiles with ideas and terminology cribbed directly from nature appears throughout this book. The purpose is to use ecosystem properties and dynamics (such as diversity) to help give direction and an over-arching sustainability perspective to the many small design and production decisions we make on a daily basis, and the hope is that we can then begin to design textile products and production systems that are as sustainable as the ecosystems they are modelled on. This chapter uses the idea of materials diversity to guide and promote the long-term health, resilience and effective-ness of the fashion and textile industry, as well as that of natural and cultural systems. Diversity is, as the saying goes, about not putting all our eggs in one basket. It avoids agricultural, manufacturing and fashion monocultures and its sustainability benefits flow from sharing ideas, spreading risk and decentraliz-ing production to maximize long-term environmental, economic and socio-cultural effectiveness and stability of the sector as a whole.

Diversity of materials and ideas is hard to find in today's fashion and textile industry. It is dominated by a large number of similar, ready-made products in a limited range of fibre types. Indeed cotton and polyester together account for over 80 per cent of the global market in textiles.[1] The result of producing large volumes of limited fibres is to concentrate impacts in specific agricul-tural or manufacturing sectors, to increase ecological risk, to make the sector less resilient to changing global conditions in both business and the environ-ment and to reduce consumer choice. Yet a sustainability-driven strategy of materials diversity doesn't require that we wipe out production of the big two fibres – far from it – more that we work to allow alternative, more resource efficient and culturally responsive fibres to flourish. Replacing some conven-tional cotton production, for example, with alternatives such as organic or low-chemical cotton, flax, hemp and lyocell could bring benefits by reducing pesticides and water use. Likewise a shift away from polyester to renewable and biodegradable fibres such as wool and those made from materials like corn starch could also bring benefits, reducing our dependency on oil. The result would be the cultivation, processing and promotion of a series of 'minority' fibres that, when taken together, amount to a majority. What is more, this majority has the potential to not only serve our material needs with reduced resource consumption, but it would also mean more varied and locally sensitive agriculture, more regional fibres, more local jobs, and more healthy and socially robust environments. Ideas of diversity rightly reflect the complexity of the relationship between fashion, textiles and sustainability. They underscore the importance of recognizing that no one fibre, regardless of whether it is organic, fairly traded or recycled, can single-handedly trans-form the practices of a polluting and resource-intensive industry into a more sustainable one. Indeed a focus on materials alone is itself never likely to achieve this.

In sustainability, there is no such thing as a single-frame approach. Issues dealt with in single frames will almost by definition lead to unwanted and unforeseen effects elsewhere. To avoid these effects we have to be aware about the impacts of our fibre choices on whole interrelated product life-cycles, which include cultivation, production, manufacturing, distribution, consumer laundering, reuse and final disposal. Focusing on the whole helps us 'scope' those lifecycle phases that are particularly high impact and iden-tify key changes that need to be made. For some textile products, such as frequently laundered clothes, for example, these key changes are linked to improved laundry practices (see Chapter 3). For other textile products such as furnishings, where the production phase is the dominant source of impact, most benefit is brought by making products last longer by, for example, using design strategies that improve both physical and emotional durability (see Chapter 7). This does not mean that choice of fibre is unimportant – on the contrary it is central to what a textile or garment is – only that it is one amid many interconnected factors influencing overall product sustainability.

With one eye firmly fixed on the bigger picture of lifecycle impacts and a goal of increasing materials diversity through our fibre choices, this chapter reviews the environmental and social impacts of fibre cultivation and produc-tion. The background to understanding the many and varied impacts of this first phase of the lifecycle is introduced, as well as a short description of the current market for textiles. The review describes some of the more 'promis-ing' fibres that are being produced. To contextualize why some are more promising than others requires us to also review the conventional ones, which is where the fibre-by-fibre analysis begins. The information contained in this chapter is by its very nature detailed and in some cases technical. It can be read from start to finish or dipped in and out of, but its purpose is the same regardless of how it is read – to provide a knowledge base about fibres from which we can begin to explore the whole system potential and direction of sustainability in the fashion and textile sector.

The market in textiles

The demand for textile fibre worldwide is increasing. Two fibres dominate this expanding market: cotton and polyester (see Table 1.1). Demand for polyester has doubled over the last 15 years, and has now overtaken cotton as the single most popular textile material. While volumes of natural fibre production have remained fairly constant for several years, demand for cotton has recently been increasing.[2]

Table 1.1 *World fibre demand in 2005*[3]

	World fibre demand (million tons)
Natural fibres	
Raw cotton	24.40
Raw wool	1.23
Raw silk	0.13
Total	25.76
Manufactured fibres	
Cellulosics	2.53
Synthetics	
Acrylic	2.63
Nylon	3.92
Polyester	24.70
Total synthetics	*31.25*
Total	33.78
TOTAL FIBRE DEMAND	59.54

Background to sustainability impacts

Surveys repeatedly show that there has been – and indeed continues to be – tremendous confusion over the sustainability impacts of producing textile materials. Synthetic fibres are commonly seen as 'bad' and natural fibres as 'good'. This preconception is influenced by a complex set of factors including raw material renewability, biodegradability and stereotyped associations made with chemicals, factories and pollution. The truth however is (as always) much more involved. While there is no dispute that producing synthetic fibres impacts on people and the environment, natural fibre cultivation and process-ing is also high impact. Cultivating 1kg of cotton for example, draws on as much as 8000 litres of water (an estimated average across the global cotton crop).[4] In comparison, producing 1kg of polyester uses little or no water. Polyester manufacture does, however, consume twice the energy needed to make the same amount of cotton. Thus the key sustainability challenges in fibre production are different for different materials. The process of recording and assessing impacts involves looking at resources consumed (energy, water, chemicals and land) and waste and emissions produced (to air, water and land). Taking the sector as a whole, the areas of greatest impact in this one lifecycle phase are:

- large quantities of water and pesticides required for growing cotton;
- emissions to air and water arising from producing synthetic and cellulosic fibres;
- adverse impacts on water linked to natural fibre production;
- significant use of energy and non-renewable resources for synthetics.

The relative importance of these impacts also has to be assessed against a constantly evolving base of scientific research and set of social and ethical concerns. For example, at the time of writing, carbon emissions have begun to dominate the sustainability debate in the UK. This has led to a rise in interest in carbon-neutral fibres (i.e. plant-based fibres that absorb the same amount of carbon dioxide from the atmosphere during their natural growth cycle as they release on harvesting) such as bamboo viscose and lyocell. Other concerns, such as rapidly reducing oil reserves and overflowing landfill sites, have meant that biodegradable fibres made from renewable resources (and particularly rapidly renewable resources (where the crop takes under three years to regrow) or annually renewable resources (crops which grow and are harvested in one year)) are increasing in popularity. This means a shift away from oil-based synthetic fibres such as polyester and nylon, which are non-renewable and non-biodegradable, to a range of natural and cellulosic fibres like cotton and lyocell, and new breeds of biodegradable synthetics made from plants, like poly(lactic acid) (PLA) from corn starch and soya bean fibre.

Fibre review

The next part of this chapter is dedicated to a review of the environmental and social impact of a range of fibres. There are two main categories of textile fibre: natural and manufactured. Natural fibres are almost exclusively made from plant or animal sources. Manufactured fibres are made from raw materials that come from a variety of sources, including plant, animal and also synthetic polymers (see Table 1.2). The following section describes some of the significant environmental impacts associated with the most popular natural and manufactured fibres. It describes resource use and impacts or emissions to air, water and land where they exist. It also provides a list of possible alternative cultivation or processing routes and material substitutes for each fibre. After the discussion of conventional fibres, a number of studies are reviewed that compare and assess fibres. This is then followed by an assessment of a wide range of more resource-efficient, 'alternative' fibres.

Table 1.2 *Textile fibre types*

Natural fibres		Manufactured fibres	
Plant	Animal	From natural polymers (vegetable and animal)	From synthetic polymers
Cotton	Wool	Regenerated cellulosic fibres	Polycondensate fibre
Linen	Silk	*Viscose*	*Polyester*
Hemp	Cashmere	*Modal*	*Nylon*
Jute	Mohair	*Lyocell*	Polymer fibre
Ramie		Alginate fibres	*Acrylic*
Sisal		*Acetate*	*Polypropylene*
Banana		*Triacetate*	*PVC*
Pineapple		Elastodiene (rubber)	
Natural bamboo		Regenerated protein fibre	
		Casein	
		Soya bean	
		Biodegradable polyester fibre	
		Poly (lactic acid) (PLA)	

Natural fibres

Cotton

The total area of land dedicated to cotton growing has not changed significantly for around 80 years, but in that time output has tripled. This hike in productivity is widely attributed to the application to the cotton crop of very large quantities of fertilizers and pesticides,[5] which in turn have caused a range of well-documented environmental impacts including: reduced soil fertility; loss of biodiversity; water pollution; pesticide-related problems including resistance; and severe health problems relating to exposure to acutely toxic pesticides.[6] Pesticides (a generic term incorporating insecticides, herbicides and fungicides) account for more than 50 per cent of the total cost of cotton production in most of the world. In cotton production, the use of insecticides dominates, with pyrethoids and organophosphates being most widely used. The World Health Organization has classified these as 'moderately hazardous'. However, some organophosphates, especially those used in developing countries, are classified as 'highly hazardous', are generally acutely toxic nerve poisons and can contaminate groundwater.[7] Large amounts of synthetic fertilizers (often based on nitrogen compounds) are also applied to the crop and can result in nitrate contamination to water, with the effect of accelerating the growth of aquatic plants and algae, and subsequent deoxygenation of water into a state in which it cannot support animal life.

The cotton crop is sometimes highly irrigated and cotton agriculture has been associated with adverse changes in water balance, the most infamous case being the 'drying up' of the Aral Sea after water was diverted from two feeding rivers to irrigate cotton plants.[8] The quantities of water needed to irrigate the cotton crop vary according to climate from as much as 29,000 litres per kg of cotton in Sudan to 7000 litres per kg in Israel.[9] However, it should be noted that 50 per cent of land under cotton cultivation is not irrigated but rain-fed, and because water cannot be 'used up' (it is circulated in a natural cycle), problems associated with high levels of water use are linked more to access to water (through wells and infrastructure) and to contamination (by fertilizers and pesticides) that makes it unfit for use for other purposes. In Central Asia, perhaps the area of most inefficiently irrigated cotton, 60 per cent of the water is lost before reaching the fields because of poor infrastructure. Furthermore, irrigation techniques in these areas are extremely inefficient, resulting in huge additional waste of water.

Other inputs in cotton cultivation include between 0.3 and 1kg of oil per kg of cotton fibre (depending on the extent to which cotton growing is mechanized) to run the farm machinery and to fuel the planes for aerial spraying.[10] If cotton is machine picked it is routinely sprayed with defoliants prior to harvesting to speed up the process, and it tends to contain considerably more impurities (seeds, dirt and plant residues) than hand-picked cotton.

Alternatives: organically grown cotton; low-chemical cotton; hand-picked cotton; rain-fed cotton; drip-irrigated cotton; substitute fibres, such as hemp or flax.

Wool

Just as in cotton production, pesticides are used in the cultivation of wool, although quantities are considerably smaller and it is thought that good practice can significantly limit any negative environmental impact. Sheep are treated either with injectable insecticides, a pour-on preparation or dipped in a pesticide bath to control parasite infection, which if left untreated can have serious welfare implications for the flock. When managed badly, these pesticides can cause harm to human health and watercourses both on the farm and in subsequent downstream processing. Organophosphates (OPs) for example, widely used in the UK until recently to treat sheep scab, are linked to severe nerve damage in humans. Their replacement, dips based on cypermethrim (a pyrethoid), while safer for farmers, has been linked to a significant growth in incidences of water pollution, as they are 1000 times more toxic to aquatic life than organophosphates. These dips now have been suspended from sale in the UK because they are linked to a high number of water pollution incidences.[11]

For almost all countries, wool is a secondary product of sheep farming – the primary product being meat. As a consequence, sheep are rarely bred for the fineness and quality of their wool and as a result the fibre, which tends to be fairly coarse, has low market value and is generally a wasted resource. An exception to this is wool from Australia's Merino sheep – the most important type of wool for apparel production. A single Merino fleece can produce around 5kg of fine, good quality wool. As the raw wool is cleaned (scoured) significant environmental impacts arise. Raw wool, like all other natural fibres, contains many impurities; it is both dirty and greasy, resulting in it being the only fibre type to require wet cleaning before yarn manufacture, although in some techniques, like Wooltech's wool cleaning system, the solvent trichloroethylene replaces the use of water. Where wool is scoured with water this is at hot temperatures to emulsify the grease. Scouring produces an effluent (wool grease sludge) with high suspended solids content and a high pollution index.[12] For each kg of scoured wool, 1.5kg of waste impurities is produced.[13] Wool grease is traditionally reclaimed from the scouring process for use as lanolin. However, pesticides applied to sheep have been found to be persistent even in refined grease, although the switch away from OP sheep dips, as well as maximizing the 'withdrawal period' (the duration of time between the last application of insecticide and scouring), is helping to reduce this.

Alternatives: choose wool scoured in factories with strict effluent treatment protocols; or if solvent scoured, where reclamation and recycling of the solvent is ensured; specify organically grown wool.

Silk

Silk is produced from the chrysalis of silkworms. Most commercially produced silk is of the cultivated variety and involves feeding the worms a carefully controlled diet of mulberry leaves grown under special conditions. Selected mulberry trees are grown to act as homes for the silkworms; their leaves are carefully picked by hand, as silk quality is highly related to a worm's diet. The trees require fertilizer and pesticides applications, although far less than cotton plants as the worms are extremely sensitive to poisoning by agrochemicals.[14] Other inputs, such as a supply of clean air and careful climate control (heating or cooling), are needed to ensure maximum yields. The fibres are extracted by steaming to kill the silk moth chrysalis (if the moth is left to emerge the silk filament is damaged) and then washed in hot water (often with detergents) to degum the silk. The waste water is usually discharged to the ground water, acting as a low level pollutant.

Alternatives: choose silk that is degummed in factories with effluent treatment protocols; specify wild silk, organic silk.

Linen

The production of linen (or flax) commonly uses agricultural chemicals and in particular fertilizers and herbicides to control weeds. However, it can grow with virtually no attention or fertilizers, as long as water is available. For top quality fibres, the climate must be very moist but mild and, as extensive irrigation is not normally required, the environmental impacts associated with water consumption, pollution and soil salinization are avoided. It is also suggested that bast fibres like linen (and also hemp, jute and kenaf) grow well on land unsuitable for food production and may help recultivate soils polluted with contaminants such as heavy metals.[15]

The selection of optimum quality flax fibre has traditionally been done by hand in many countries – something that makes the process more financially costly, though having environmental benefits. The customary process of degumming flax fibres from the stalk (retting) involves placing small bundles of stalks in water tanks, open retting ponds or running river water, while the stalk rots and the fibres are separated from the woody core.[16] The nutrients from the decaying stalks mean that water retting is highly polluting to water. Best practice involves alternative techniques such as dew retting (where plants are left to decompose on the ground with the right conditions of heat and moisture) and enzyme retting (in which enzymes are applied to the flax either in the field or in tanks), which avoid pollution problems associated with the traditional method. Indeed, as part of the push to reduce the environmental impact of retting and increase mechanization, there is a trend towards the development of a number of mechanical treatments for processing flax and other bast fibres so that they become more similar to cotton in their properties and can be processed on equipment designed for cotton.

Alternatives: dew-retted flax; substitute fibres such as hemp.

Manufactured fibres

Polyester

The agents used in the manufacture of polyester are petrochemicals, and arguably its chief impacts stem from the political, social and pollution effects of the petrochemical industry. Chief among them is the high ecological and social cost of oil exploration and extraction and the vast network of pipes and other infrastructure necessary to transport the oil to the big oil-consuming nations. In the production of polyester, the main chemicals used are terephthalic acid (TA) or dimethyl terephthalate, which are reacted with ethylene glycol. The dominant route for polyester fibre manufacture involves a process of purifying TA and is based on bromide-controlled oxidation. Petroleum products are not only used as feedstock, but are also used to generate the energy required to convert the fibre. The amount of energy consumed in producing 1kg of polyester is 109 megajoules (MJ), the product of 46MJ of fuel value of the crude oil and natural gas used for making the raw materials and 63MJ of energy needed to process this raw material into fibre.[17]

In general terms, water consumption in the production of manufactured fibres is lower than for natural fibres. Polyester for example, can be processed by several routes; the most common one, described above, consumes 'small amounts' of water, although in other routes no water is consumed.[18] Emissions (to air and water) arising from the production of polyester that are seen to have a medium to high potential for causing environmental damage, if discharged untreated, include: heavy metal cobalt; manganese salts; sodium bromide; antimony oxide (which is licensed by law despite it being a known carcinogen); and titanium dioxide.

Alternatives: choose fabrics not made with catalytic agents containing cobalt or manganese salts and those that avoid antimony based catalysts; specify recycled polyester; choose fibre substitutes such as PLA.

Nylon

Similarly to polyester, nylon (or polyamide) fibres are based on a petrochemical feedstock and are affected by the same issues, namely the political, ecological and pollution effects associated with carbon chemistry. There are several forms of nylon. In the production of nylon 6.6 for example, raw materials including hexamethylendiamine and adipic acid are combined to form a polyamide salt. The molecules of the two chemicals react under high pressure and heat. The polymer is then extracted and cooled with water. While details of the production sequence for nylon fibres are well documented,[19] information or analysis of its environmental impacts is not in the public domain. The process is known to be energy intensive, however, and producing 1kg of fabric consumes 150MJ (as compared with 109MJ per kg for polyester and 50MJ per kg for cotton).[20] Producing nylon also produces emissions of nitrous oxide, a potent greenhouse gas. Nitrous oxide emissions from a single UK nylon plant in the 1990s were thought to have a global warming impact equivalent to more than 3 per cent of the UK's entire carbon dioxide emissions.[21]

Alternatives: Substitute alternative fibres such as wool (for example in carpets).

Acrylic

Like other synthetic fibres, acrylic fibres are made from mineral oil or other hydrocarbons. Acrylic polymer is produced by forcing acrylonitrile to react with various combinations of process chemicals including styrene, vinyl acetate, ammonium persulphate and iron, among others. It is then solvent spun, washed in hot water to remove residual solvents and salts, drawn in tanks of water that are kept near boiling point (to give the fibre strength), finished by immersion in an acid bath to give the fibre an anti-static treatment and then dried. Acrylic is 30 per cent more energy intensive in its production than polyester (1kg of acrylic fibre consumes 157MJ) and consumes substantially more water.[22] The environmental implications of its production are not well understood, though it is thought that a significant number of production chemicals (including its base ingredient acrylonitrile) have a high potential for creating environmental problems if discharged untreated.

Alternatives: avoid acrylic fibres and fabrics processed with vinyl acetate and those spun with the solvent dimethylformamide; substitute alternatives such as wool.

Viscose

Cellulosic fibres like viscose are formed from natural polymers that are chemically dissolved and then extruded as a continuous filament. A common source of cellulose for viscose is fast-growing softwoods such as beech, although other sources such as bamboo have gained in popularity more recently. The raw material for cellulosic fibres is frequently described as carbon neutral (where the growing cycle of the plant absorbs the same amount of carbon dioxide from the atmosphere as it gives out on harvesting). However, the rest of the viscose fibre production process has significant environmental implications. The cellulose is first purified and bleached and then soaked in sodium hydroxide. It is then treated with carbon disulphide and finally spun in a solution of sulphuric acid, sodium sulphate, zinc sulphate and glucose.[23] The production of viscose generates emissions to air in the form of sulphur, nitrous oxides, carbon disulphide and hydrogen sulphide. Emissions from the process to water result in high pollution indexes. These emissions are all considered to have major potential for creating environmental problems if discharged untreated. One study of the toxicity of viscose water effluents concluded: 'It had high levels of bio-chemically degradable substances, organic matter, nitrates, phosphates, iron, zinc, oil and grease. The effluent was completely devoid of dissolved oxygen and micro organisms.'[24]

Alternatives: viscose made from wood from sustainably managed forests; viscose produced without chlorine-containing bleach and zinc sulphate and which avoids catalytic agents containing cobalt or manganese; choose viscose from factories with strict effluent treatment protocols including biological purification before discharge; substitute viscose for lyocell (trade name Tencel).

Fibre comparisons and assessments

As the previous part of this chapter has highlighted, sustainability issues associated with fibres are complex, with many trade-offs, making findings difficult to interpret. To help us in this task, there are a range of different tools, software models and methods that we can use. Some of these are based on qualitative assessments with the aim of gathering basic information about key issues; others quantify and balance a product's environmental impacts, frequently using a technique called lifecycle assessment (LCA). Both approaches have limitations. For example, qualitative studies tend to generate equivocal findings. And LCAs, even though there are well-established internationally recognized methodologies, have a history of partisan results and methodological inconsistencies arising from different ways of defining boundaries around the problem being investigated.[25] So the same rules apply to interpreting findings about fibre impacts as to analysing all information: use multiple sources and check data for impartiality. For all this, fibre assessments and comparisons are extremely valuable and are perhaps at their most powerful when they are used to drive new ideas and innovation forward. They can do this by highlighting particularly polluting or resource-intensive practices, and so act as a spur to drive change towards low-impact methods and, when used as part of a creative process, to assess the sustainability potential of alternative scenarios and future strategies.

Fibre assessments and comparisons have also been used in other ways, including to defend a company's products, frequently by shifting the spotlight of environmental impact onto other fibres (usually cotton). In the early 1990s for example, the synthetic fibre producer DuPont published a rank of a range of fibres that,[26] it claimed, covered the whole lifecycle (although the report said little about assessment criteria, methodology or assumptions). It concluded that polypropylene is the preferred fibre; followed by nylon; joint third position is held by wool, polyester and acrylic; cotton is in sixth place, and viscose is given the worst environmental loading. Also in the 1990s, cellulosics fibre producer Lenzing published comparisons, contrasting viscose and cotton, concluding that viscose causes slightly less impact.[27] In another comparison, this time of cotton and lyocell, Lenzing concludes that cotton uses more agrochemicals, land and water than the lyocell and only slightly less energy.[28] Cynically, these studies can be seen as an attempt to deflect scrutiny from these manufacturers' own products at a time when manufactured fibres were widely perceived as 'bad' for the environment. Yet these studies also hint at the beginnings of an awareness of a more complex and relational understanding of sustainability issues associated with textile fibres, an understanding that has since been promoted by a wide range of other studies.

While not a comparative study per se, the Danish Environmental Protection Agency's report *Environmental Assessment of Textiles*[29] discusses a wide range of lifecycle impacts (in qualitative and quantitative terms) associated with a range of textile fibres. Data from the report on water and energy consumption associated with the fibre cultivation/extraction phase of five fibre types is set out in Figure 1.1. The high figure for water use in cotton cultivation is an estimated average across the global cotton crop.[30] Perhaps most usefully, the chart underscores the extent of variations in resource consumption for this single lifecycle phase on just two criteria and reiterates the

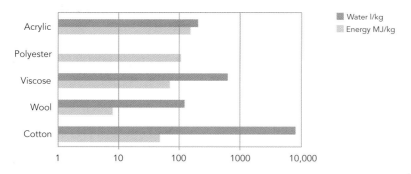

Figure 1.1 *Energy and water consumption in the production of selected fibre types (note the log scale)*[31]

message that all fibres cause an impact in their cultivation/extraction phase. For viscose, acrylic and polyester there are also significant emissions to air; for viscose and wool significant emissions to water; and for cotton very high levels of pesticide use. Other phases of the lifecycle, including manufacturing, use and disposal, also consume resources and produce wastes and in many cases these environmental impacts dwarf those associated with fibre cultivation and production.

Other authors have used the process of comparing fibres to predict future fibre trends and market success. One such study,[32] published in 1996, contrasted the environmental costs of producing three 'alternative' fibres: hemp, lyocell and recycled polyester. Its conclusion states that in the short term waste products (such as recycled polyester) will be popular, and in the medium term lyocell will be successful. Hemp is the only fibre of the three seen to have 'true environment friendliness' and, if its association with marijuana production is controlled, it is considered the most successful of the three in both environmental and market terms 'once raw material scarcity has reduced our ability to produce the other two fibres'. Ten years on from the publication of this study, 'raw material scarcity' is yet to bite; however, interest in renewable resource based fibres (including lyocell, bamboo, PLA and soya bean) is growing and these are frequently promoted as replacements for petrochemical-derived synthetic fibres like polyester. Regardless, all of these fibres continue to remain niche products, none of them having won a substantial market share. Instead, perhaps the most familiar 'alternative' fibre is organic cotton.

Organic cotton is the focus of another comparative study,[33] this time with an affiliation to the company Patagonia, which has a strong interest in the fibre. Here the environmental costs for growing cotton conventionally are

Table 1.3 *Environmental cost of each stage in the lifecycle of a cotton T-shirt (US dollars per T-shirt)*[34]

	Conventional cotton	Organic cotton
Growing	0.67	0.33
Ginning	0.02	0.02
Processing	0.02	0.02
Distribution	0.08	0.08
Transportation	0.32	0.32
Consumer care	2.69	2.69
Total	$3.79	$3.45

contrasted with growing it organically. This study converted the costs into a monetary value, priced per stage in the lifecycle (see Table 1.3). They show that the environmental costs of growing conventional cotton are roughly twice those of organic cotton. This variation reflects differences between the two techniques' effects on soil erosion, their pesticide use and water consumption. It is worth noting, however, that the most impact is attributed to the consumer care phase of the lifecycle (discussed further below).

The significant role played by consumer practice in a textile product's overall lifecycle performance was first highlighted by an LCA of a polyester blouse conducted in 1993 by Franklin Associates for the American Fiber Manufacturers Association.[35] Its conclusions state that as much as 82 per cent of energy use, 66 per cent of solid waste, 'over half' of the emissions to air and 'large quantities' of waterborne effluents produced throughout the product lifecycle are amassed during use phase of the lifecycle (i.e. laundering) (see Chapter 3 – Use Matters). Rather than comparing different fibres, this study compares the impact of lifecycle phases internal to a product with a view to identifying areas where change would bring most benefit.

LCA-driven data also plays a prominent role in the University of Cambridge report *Well Dressed?*[36] In the report, impacts arising from different scenarios for three textile products are compared. For each scenario, the product's impact is compared against the impact of the 'base case', so as to identify increases or reductions in impact. The report focuses on a cotton T-shirt, viscose blouse and nylon carpet, and compares environmental, economic and social data for various scenarios, including:

-      changing the location of textile and clothing operations with and without new production technology and recycling schemes;
-      changing consumer behaviour including extending the life of clothing and improving the efficiency of laundering practices;
-      introducing alternative fibres, green manufacturing and 'smart' technologies.

The results show that shifting production of the T-shirt and viscose blouse to the UK brings modest savings across the board. The savings are modest only, because the use of energy for transportation is relatively small (compared to the washing of clothes) so shifting location of production has little effect. In contrast, changing consumer behaviour and particularly omitting tumble-drying can have a large positive effect on environmental impact. A positive effect on social impact is also possible if consumers change behaviour and embrace a raft of reuse, repair and recycling activities to enhance the lifespan of their clothes. The introduction of alternative fibres and innovative tech-nologies such as organic cotton and stain-repellent coatings in the case of the T-shirt brings savings across all measures. For carpets, however, switching from man-made to natural fibres has mixed effects, generating more carbon dioxide and waste but fewer other environmental impacts such as ozone depletion, acidification, nutrient enrichment and smog formation. Not only is the detail provided by this report very useful, its whole approach – based on lifecycles, industrial systems and recommendations that stretch beyond traditional company boundaries to also include consumers – is progressive. Usefully from a design perspective, it also shows how scenario building can be used creatively to imagine a different future for the fashion and textile sector.

Fibre 'alternatives'

The process of reviewing and comparing fibres makes opportunities to reduce impact more visible. These include, for example, the development of better practices in the production of conventional fibres as well as the introduction of a group of different and inherently lower-impact fibres. Some of these changes could be brought about by a move to alternative systems of agriculture that are already well established (integrated pest management or organic cultivation methods, for example), while others are more challenging and need technical development. The following section reviews a wide range of these alternatives.

Organic cotton

The greatest sustainability challenges for cotton cultivation lie in reducing pesticide, fertilizer and water use and promoting better information and conditions for farmers. Cultivating cotton organically, that is in a system that does not use synthetic pesticides, fertilizers, growth regulators or defoliants, addresses many of these issues. In the organic system the use of synthetic pesticides and fertilizers is avoided, as natural methods are used to control pests, weeds and disease. Particular attention is paid to the use of locally adapted varieties, the reduction of nutrient losses through wide crop rotation and mechanical and manual weed control.[37] Switching to organic production brings a major reduction in the toxicity profile for cotton (as minimal chemicals are used). Table 1.4 shows the lifecycle toxicity profile for a conventionally grown cotton T-shirt. Organic production results in a dramatic change in the profile – the toxicity of the materials cultivation phase of the lifecycle drops to zero and overall product toxicity is reduced by 93 per cent.[38]

Organic production also has a strong social element and includes many Fair Trade and ethical production principles[40] – as such it can be seen as more than a set of agricultural practices, but also as a tool for social change. For example, one of the original undertakings of the organic movement was to create speciality products for small farmers, who would then receive a premium for their products and allow them to compete with large commercial farms. Further promoting social change, organic standards also make recommendations to industry about production. The view is that it is not enough for cotton to be grown organically and then processed in a conventional, polluting system. In some organic textile standards and accreditation

Table 1.4 *Toxicity profile of a conventionally grown cotton T-shirt[39]*

Lifecycle phase	Percentage of total impact
Material	93.0
Production	3.5
Transportation	1.0
Use	2.5
Disposal	0.0

◄ Eco jeans
in 100 per
cent organic
cotton with
sustainable
product
components
and
production
processes by
Levi's

schemes, such as that provided by the Soil Association in the UK,[41] lists of permitted process chemicals and recommendations for dyeing and finishing techniques are included. Accreditation is increasingly popular and is linked to the success of organically grown food. As well as a host of small companies producing fully accredited organic cotton ranges, large corporates, like Levi's, have produced an organic cotton jean, and Nike and Marks and Spencer have pledged to blend 5 per cent organic cotton into all their cotton products by 2010.

Unlike more politically contentious and technically challenging 'alternative' fibres such as hemp, organic cotton fibre is a fairly straightforward like-for-like substitute for conventionally grown cotton and as such it has been fairly quickly incorporated into existing product lines. The main factor limiting the increased use of organic cotton is its limited supply. Presently, organic cotton makes up a tiny percentage (0.18 per cent) of world fibre demand and around 1 per cent of the total cotton market. More farmers are converting to fully accredited organic production; however, the process is slow (taking three years), costly and is a risky venture for many farmers who are already struggling to stay on the land. The quality of cotton grown in organic systems is equal to that grown in conventional ones; however, uniformity over large volumes can be an issue due to the limited supply of organic fibre for blending. Productivity of organic production is usually less than for conventional production, by up to 50 per cent, and this has given rise to scepticism in the fibre industry about organic cotton's viability as a true replacement for conventionally grown fibre, as lower yields require more land (of which there is a finite amount) in order to meet demand.

Low-chemical cotton

Organic methods of cultivation offer one way to reduce the use of chemicals in cotton production, although other methods exist such as integrated pest management and the introduction of genetically modified (GM) varieties. In California, USA, it has been found that biological integrated pest management (IPM) techniques have the potential to reduce chemical use by more than that acheived by organic cultivation practices. They do this by bringing more farmers and more hectares into chemically reduced programmes and so reducing chemical use across a large numbers of farms rather than just eliminating it in a few.[42] In California, organic cultivation of cotton has been slow to take off because of the method's increased demand for manual labour, which makes Californian-grown organic fibre expensive. The Sustainable Cotton Project has championed IPM techniques in California through its BASIC (biological agricultural systems in cotton) programme, and claims that over the last seven years BASIC growers have consistently achieved reduction of fungicides, insecticides and miticides by around 70 per cent.[43] BASIC cotton is also non-GM and is recommended by the Sustainable Cotton Project as a complement to organic programmes.

A very different low-chemical approach to BASIC is offered by the introduction of GM varieties of cotton. Whereas organic and non-GM agricultural programmes like BASIC engage farmers in biological solutions to pest management and natural agricultural controls, GM is a technological or industrial 'fix' to chemical reduction. Recent figures suggest that GM cotton now represents 21 per cent of the global market in cotton[44] and is grown in nine countries. The main varieties of GM cotton grown assist with pest management (and include the bacterial toxin *Bacillus thuringiensis* (Bt)) or are tolerant to herbicides (HT), although varieties with multiple traits are now available. For farmers the benefits of GM varieties include: reduced pesticide use (because the crop comes under attack less often); equal or higher yields; no impact on fibre quality; and increased income (because of less outlay on pesticides).[45] For the environment, chief benefits arise through reduced pesticide use. For example, it is claimed that significant reductions in pesticides use has occurred in every country where Bt cotton has been grown. Moreover, it leads to low tillage of the soil, which leads to less particulate matter in the air and greater water retention due to less compacted soil.[46] There are, however, a number of concerns about GM agriculture. One report, by the biotech industry itself, revealed that while pesticide use did decline in the first three years after herbicide tolerant GM crops were commercialized, it is now significantly higher than on conventional crops.[47] This is explained by weed communities changing to species that are more tolerant of high doses of herbicide, which has resulted in farmers spraying more. However, perhaps the greatest concern of GM technology is that its rapid rise (GM crops were introduced for the first time in 1996) is driven by commercial gain and the goal of making marketable products rather than long-term ecological or social improvements. Interestingly, the Better Cotton Initiative (BCI),[48] a body made up of representatives of the cotton supply chain from farmers to retailers, whose aim is to balance the environmental, social and economic sustainability of cotton cultivation on a large scale, has not rejected GM-cotton in its standards, instead choosing to review the efficacy of a range of approaches on a region-by-region and case-by-case basis.

Low water use cotton

In addition to reducing the chemical use of cotton, minimizing water usage of cotton also brings benefits. Around 50 per cent of cotton is irrigated; the remainder is partially irrigated or depends entirely on rainwater. Currently, 99 per cent of West African cotton is rain-fed, as is a large proportion of Indian cotton. Rain-fed cotton offers obvious benefits including healthier soils and less demand on the water infrastructure, although there are trade-offs. Though it uses less water, rain-fed cotton also tends to be of poorer quality because of the sporadic water to the plant. Efficient irrigation techniques are also available, such as drip irrigation that reportedly saves up to 30 per cent water consumption compared to conventional irrigation.[49] This technique, however, is labour intensive and only suitable to areas where hand picking is the harvesting method, as the drip irrigation lines have to be laid down by hand and in any country that harvests mechanically these have to be ripped up at the end of the growing season.

Fair Trade cotton

There are many social and health issues associated with cotton cultivation, including poor workers' rights (low pay, lack of job security, etc.) and hazardous working conditions (mainly associated with application of pesticides). While most organic or low-chemical schemes tend to concentrate on environmental standards, other initiatives work to improve the sustainability of cotton agriculture by focusing on social goals. One such example is the Fair Trade movement, which aims to ensure that producers receive a fair price for their product, benefit from acceptable working conditions and have access to education and healthcare. In 2005, a Fairtrade mark was introduced for seed cotton[50] (the raw cotton, before ginning) that guarantees that cotton growers earn a minimum price for their product and a further premium to be used for community development projects. It also includes some environmental criteria and seeks to minimize the use of agrochemicals and prohibit the use of the most hazardous pesticides. Fairtrade mark cotton farmers are also required to use individual protective equipment when spraying pesticides, to help reduce the risk of pesticide poisoning.[51] Notably, Marks and Spencer has committed to producing 20 million garments in Fairtrade mark cotton by 2008 as part of its 'Plan A' sustainability initiative. Other projects, such as Indian based Agrocel or Illuminati II,[52] a sister company of high end brand Noir, produce high quality fairly traded African cotton based on the United Nation's Global Compact Principles,[53] which include labour, human rights, environment and anti-corruption issues.

◀ White 100 per
cent African
cotton dress
by Noir

Organic wool

Organic wool comes from sheep reared on organically grown feed, that graze
on land not treated with pesticides and that are not dipped in synthetic
pyrethoids or OPs. Sheep scab can be controlled only with certain injectable
or pour-on preparations that minimize use of chemicals, impacts on fresh
water ecology and downstream processing. While the market for organic
wool is very small, it is growing, given impetus by companies like Marks and
Spencer, who as part of its 'Plan A' sustainability initiative is sourcing a range
of more sustainable fibres, including organic wool. Organically grown wool
fibre can now be processed in the UK into a fully licensed organic product
(which requires each manufacturing stage to have separate organic accreditation) and Isle of Mull Weavers has produced the UK's first organic tweed.[54]

Hemp

Hemp (sometimes called cannabis hemp) grows very rapidly, naturally smoth-
ering weeds and controlling pests, and so is thought to be suited to low-
impact systems of agriculture. Growing hemp also helps clear land for other
crops; it improves the structure of the soil, its strong roots controlling erosion;
it has a high yield and can be grown in cool climates. It grows to between one
and four metres tall and yields around six tonnes per hectare. Between 20
and 30 per cent of the plant is fibre and its productivity is far superior to other
natural fibres (see Table 1.5). This leads to claims that hemp gives a 'double
dividend': a reduction in the ecological footprint of production by about half,
if grown to replace cotton for use in textiles, and wood for use in the pulp
and paper industries.[55]

    The narcotic properties of hemp have meant that its cultivation is banned
in many countries. Varieties with a low psychoactive compound Tetrahydo-
cannabinol (THC) have been introduced and are now grown, including in the
UK, though very little is processed into fibre. Fibre extraction and associated
environmental problems are similar to those for flax (i.e. by retting). Optimum
quality fibre is achieved by using traditional hand methods of harvesting and
processing (still done in some parts of China); however, high labour costs
make this uneconomic in many countries. As a result other fibre extraction
techniques have been developed and include enzyme retting and steam
explosion. In steam explosion the fibre and the hemp plant's woody core are
broken apart by a blast of steam and this shortens the fibre's staple length.
While this makes hemp easier to process on the most common cotton spinning system, it reduces its strength.

Table 1.5 *Average natural fibre production per hectare*

	Average fibre production (kg) per hectare
Cotton	300–1100
Flax	800–1150
Hemp	1200– 2000
Wool	62

Wild (tussah or peace) silk

Wild or tussah silk production cultivates silkworms in open forest, where there is an easy source of food, and uses no hazardous chemicals. As such its production can encourage forest preservation (as an integral part of the forest ecosystem) and provide a major year-round income for millions of tribal people in India.[56] The silkworm chrysalis is collected after the moth has emerged naturally (as compared with cultivated silk, where the silkworm grub is killed while in situ), hence the term 'peace' or sometimes 'vegetarian' silk. It is then degummed in the same way as cultivated silk by washing with mild detergent. Wild silk is of lower quality than cultivated silk as the moth damages the silk cocoon as it exits the chrysalis, breaking the single continuous filament. Thus wild silk yarn and fabric, unlike that from cultivated silk, is made from short lengths of fibre (or staples) and is spun in a similar way to other staple fibres such as cotton.[57]

Poly(lactic acid)

Poly(lactic acid) (PLA) is a thermoplastic polyester (an entirely new class of synthetic fibre, sometimes called biopolymers) derived from 100 per cent renewable sources, presently corn. Unlike conventional synthetics like polyester, which is made from fossil fuels and is non-biodegradable, PLA fibre is derived from annually renewable crops and is compostable, although only in industrial composting facilities that provide the right combination of temperature and humidity to trigger the fibre to break down.[58] While claims about the sustainability benefits of biopolymers over petrochemical fibres include energy savings, fewer emissions and use of renewable resources, they are also associated with significant environmental impacts. These include the negative effects associated with large-scale, intensive agriculture and the problems associated with landfilled biopolymers with the generation of methane, a powerful greenhouse gas. As a result there have been some calls for a full assessment of the impact of biopolymers on sustainability indicators of land use, soil conservation and nutrient cycles as well as the more established indicators such as greenhouse gas emissions and energy flows.[59]

Initial uses of PLA were limited to biomedical applications such as suture material because of the high cost of manufacture and limited availability. However, more recently, economic large-scale operations have developed (such as by NatureWorks LLC), although it is still over three times more expensive than polyester.[60] PLA is created by extracting starch from the corn, converting it to sugar by enzymatic hydrolysis and then to lactic acid through fermentation. This is then turned into fibre using traditional melt spinning equipment and processes. For the NatureWorks plant, corn is the cheapest and most readily available source of sugar. However, the use of US-grown corn as the raw material for NatureWorks' product (Ingeo) has meant that

▼ Bette hemp dress by Enamore

▲ Woven fabric in 100 per cent peace silk by Denise Bird Woven Textiles

it has been unable to guarantee a GM-free status of the fibre, because of the US policy of not segregating its GM and non-GM corn crops. This has resulted in pioneering sustainability companies, like Patagonia for example, refusing to use Ingeo on the grounds that it could contain some GM parent materials. NatureWorks is now working towards third party certification to guarantee GM-free fibre.[61] There are alternatives to corn for the starch or sugar supply. With some technical development to fermentation techniques and PLA production, other non-food crops such as grass and even biomass could be used.

PLA can be produced as both filament and spun yarn. Fabrics from spun yarn have a 'natural' hand, considered to feel similar to cotton, whereas fabrics from filament yarn have a cool and soft hand and high drape. Its fibre properties can be considered broadly similar to polyester; however, it has a lower melting point, which can restrict its use in certain applications, make it unsuitable for certain processing routes (such as transfer printing) and, most critically, means it can't be ironed. This is particularly problematic for consumer aftercare of garments, which is notoriously difficult for manufacturers to control. At ironing temperatures suitable for cotton or polyester, today's commercially available PLA fibres begin to melt. Another restriction arises in dyeing and finishing – where water can enter the fibre and weaken the molecular

bonds and reduce fibre strength if appropriate processing (most notably cool temperature and acid) conditions are not observed. This is problematic in bleaching and dyeing, as these tend to use alkaline processes. Further, when dyeing PLA, more dye is wasted than when dyeing polyester. Dark shades are difficult to obtain because of these lower dye exhaustion levels – although these technical difficulties are predicted to be resolved over time. Some research has indicated that PLA is more sustainable than comparable polymers on the market today.[62]

Lyocell

Lyocell is a cellulosic fibre made from wood pulp, normally eucalyptus, and was developed in the 1980s as, it is claimed, 'an environmentally responsible fibre utilising renewable resources as its raw materials'.[63] The wood pulp is dissolved in a solution of amine oxide (a solvent) that is then spun into fibres and the solvent extracted as the fibres pass through a washing process. Other than evaporation of water, the manufacturing process recovers 99.5 per cent of the solvent, which is purified and then recycled back into the main process.

▲ T-shirt in 100 per cent Ingeo produced as part of the 'Genetic Modification' collection by Moral Fervor, inspired by the quandary surrounding GM technology

► Suit in lyocell by Linda Loudermilk

The solvent itself is non-toxic, non-corrosive and all the effluent produced is non-hazardous. Lyocell has other environmental benefits, including its full biodegradability (taking six weeks in an aerated compost heap), its renewable raw material (eucalyptus has a fast growing cycle and reaches maturity in seven years), and the fact that careful attention is paid to sourcing wood pulp from fully accredited sustainably managed forests. Further environmental advantages include: no bleaching prior to processing as the fibre is already 'very clean'; reduced chemical, water and energy consumption in dyeing; and effective low temperature laundering.

While the process of lyocell production consumes few other resources, it is energy intensive. One manufacturer, Lenzing, cites tackling energy use as one of its future challenges.[64] An ongoing challenge is to contain the tendency of lyocell fibres to crease and 'fibrillate' in the wet state (i.e. for small fibre-like structures to peel away from the main body of the fibre but remain attached). Early versions of lyocell were typified by a creased and fuzzy or 'peach skin' fabric aesthetic with white lines and damage marks on the finished goods, limiting its market appeal. Developments such as an enzyme treatment to remove the fibrils (which are first deliberately induced by a mechanical or peroxide bleach treatment) or the application of a resin to prevent fibrillation being generated in domestic washing have begun to address this. As with all similar processes, these consume a combination of energy and chemical inputs and produce waste and emissions.

Bamboo

Bamboo fibre is made of cellulose derived from the fast-growing and typically woody bamboo grass. There are two types of fibre available: natural bamboo (sometimes called bamboo 'linen' because of its hand and drape) that is extracted directly from bamboo culms; and bamboo viscose (which is by far the most common), where bamboo is substituted for beech as the source of raw cellulose in viscose production. There is limited information available about the processing route for natural bamboo fibre and it appears its commercial production is at present limited to a single company in China, apparently not using any chemical additives in processing,[65] although there is little evidence to validate this claim. Bamboo viscose is processed using the same (high) impact route as conventional viscose, although it does have the benefit of being sourced from a very rapidly regenerating raw material. It is worth noting, however, that even a vigorous and abundant plant like bamboo still has to be harvested in a sustainable way to get maximum ecological benefit.

▶ Black dress in bamboo viscose by Linda Loudermilk

There are many claims made of bamboo fibres, including health-giving properties like natural antibacterial resistance; however, cellulose is not inherently antimicrobial and there is nothing in the production process of viscose that could render fibres antimicrobial, so there is little evidence for this. Bamboo fabrics generally have other favourable characteristics, including good moisture transmission, drape and efficient colouration.

Soya

Soya fibres are part of a class of regenerated materials made from protein either from a vegetable (like soya beans) or animal (like milk, fibre name casein) source.[66] They were initially developed in the 1950s and recently have undergone a renaissance as ecological pressure to develop fully biodegradable fibres from renewable sources has intensified. In the 1950s the fibres were viewed as substitutes for more traditional ones in a time of shortages after World War II but were shelved due to technical difficulties and intense competition from other fibres (both natural and synthetic). Recent research and development, conducted mainly in the US and China, has overcome some of these difficulties and has produced a fibre with a soft handle and attractive lustre, similar to that of silk. Soya fibre is seen as a potential replacement for petrochemical-based synthetics generally and also for cashmere. China, a world leader in cashmere production, hopes that soya fibres, sometimes called 'vegetable cashmere', can help reduce the negative impact caused by cashmere goats grazing on fragile grassland.

The developments that have led to the commercial production of soya fibres involve bioengineering techniques to modify the soya bean protein's structure, using enzymes and incorporating polyvinyl alcohol either into the spinning solution or as a central core surrounded by an outer coating of soya protein to add strength and acceptable wearability characteristics to the fibre. The agents used in the processing of soya bean fibre are said to be non-toxic and waste can be used as animal feed once the protein has been extracted. Like bamboo, soya fibres are promoted as health-giving with natural antibacterial properties, although as with bamboo there is no evidence available to support this claim. Perhaps the biggest concern relating to soya fibres is related to the environmental impact of soya bean agriculture. Commercial, large-scale soya bean farming is water, fertilizer and pesticide intensive, and is commonly reliant on GM technology and widespread herbicide use supported by biotechnology companies. Some soya fibres are marketed with organic certification and these are currently around 30 per cent more expensive than organic cotton.

Naturally coloured fibre

Naturally coloured fibre takes advantage of colour variations in natural fibre types (notably cotton and wool), growing a coloured fibre that is not bleached or dyed, so avoiding the impacts associated with colouration. Naturally pigmented or 'native' cottons were conserved by traditional peoples and have a colour range of 8 to 12 shades of beige, red, earth brown, chocolate brown and green.[67] There are a number of problems associated with these cotton varieties, such as short staple and fineness, that has limited their appeal. Yet these fibres have continued to be developed in a number of projects, such as in Peru with Naturtex Partners,[68] which involves many small indigenous producers using organic methods.

Recycled fibre

Recycled fibre offers a low-impact alternative to other fibre sources, with reduced energy consumption, reduced resource consumption and reduced chemical consumption if the fibre is not over-dyed. For example, in a recycled pure wool fabric, energy consumption is thought to be half that needed to produce virgin material.[69] While most textiles can be recycled, in the main they are downgraded almost immediately into low-quality end-uses, such as filling materials. The limited range of recycled materials available reflects the market dominance of cheap virgin fibres and the lack of technological innovation in the recycling industry. For 200 years recycling technology has stayed the same; fibres are extracted from used fabric by mechanically tearing the fabric apart using carding machines. The process breaks the fibres, producing much shortened lengths that tend to make a low quality yarn. Innovation to extract longer fibres and develop quality products could work to change this. Small-scale ventures such as Annie Sherburne's recycled London textile yarn are part of this change.[70]

Textiles made from synthetic fibres can also be recycled chemically in a process that involves breaking down the fibre at the molecular level and then re-polymerizing the feedstock. While chemical recycling is more energy intensive than mechanical pulling, the resulting fibre tends to be of more predictable quality. The most commonly available recycled synthetic fibre is polyester made from plastic bottles, although recycled nylon is also available. Repreve by Unifi[71] is one example of a recycled synthetic fibre and is a 100 per cent recycled polyester yarn made from both post-consumer and post-industrial waste that can be dyed at the spun fibre stage. It has applications that range from home furnishings through to automotive upholstery, and is used by

Malden Mills for its recycled content Polartec-branded polyester garments[72] (see Chapter 4).

Moving forward

The environmental and social impacts of producing textiles are many and varied and expose a mosaic of interconnected resource flows that underpin even our simplest design choices. Our first task is to acknowledge this complexity in our work and to build expertise with a portfolio of more sustainable fibres chosen because of their appropriateness to product and user. Indeed, perhaps one of the greatest challenges of sustainability is to become skilled at this task. This allows us to become comfortable with the complexity of sustainability issues in fashion and textiles; to soak them up, yet not feel disempowered. Our holy grail is to be able to translate knowledge of 'big picture' issues (like diversity, ethics or consumption), and 'small picture' detail (such as a fibre's LCA profile) and still be able to make decisions that are simple,

▲ Yarn made from 50 per cent recycled London textiles and 50 per cent pure new wool by EcoAnnie

practical and insightful. This relies as much on traditional design skills, like experience and intuition, as on 'science', and we must learn to combine our skills in new ways.

The fashion and textile industry's future success will depend on us reducing its environmental and social burden across the entire lifecycle. Part of this is reducing the impact associated with cultivating and producing all textile fibres and establishing a foundation of good practice across the board – a major ongoing challenge. Another part involves developing a new and more sustainable way of thinking about materials that helps us move away from a dependency on a few fibres, to developing a portfolio of fibres, some with low resource intensity, others with rich cultural traditions, and all which celebrate the range of skills, know-how and resources that are available to us. This strategy of materials diversity involves replacing some of the dominant or high impact fibres with alternatives, including low-chemical and organic cotton, hemp, lyocell, wool and PLA. This would help us pursue multiple strategies to tackle sustainability problems. There is, after all, no single one-size-fits-all sustainability solution but multiple design opportunities working at different scales, levels and timeframes, and with many different people. In nature, this sort of diversity leads to strong, resilient ecosystems, able to withstand a shock or period of crisis. In fashion and textiles, it similarly could lead to a healthier and more robust industry that would support and regenerate smaller scale industry that still exists in places like Europe and India as well as reaping the rewards of efficient large-scale production in the big mills of the USA and China. Our task is to follow nature's lead and diversify while cooperating. Material diversity does, however, come at a financial price – producing small-scale fibres at multiple locations near to markets translates into more expensive fashion and textile products – and this will be passed on to consumers. As such its success would depend on reversing the general trend of higher volumes and falling prices, as typified by retailers such as Primark and Matalan, and convincing consumers to buy differently.

It is naive to think that fibre alternatives as varied as wild silk, soya bean and naturally coloured cotton can make inroads into established textile markets overnight. Their volumes are small, their cultivation and processing technologies in need of major research and development, and their long-term impacts untested. Novel fibres like these are exciting, they can play a part in more sustainable product development and also promote a debate about a shift in consumption away from quantity and towards quality (see Chapter 5). However, in searching for novelty we can sometimes disregard the familiar and lose sight of the major improvements being made to more conventional fibres. Change is best promoted by asking questions of fibres and by letting suppliers inform us about the sustainability profile of their products. We need to ask about raw materials, processing chemicals, emissions, recyclability and biodegradability. We need to ask about what is most appropriate for our product and what helps people the most. We need to be informed about fibre impacts and possibilities and we must design with a more pluralistic, decentralized and diverse view of what our industry can be.

CHAPTER TWO Ethically Made

Producing fashion and textiles involves one of the longest and most com-
plicated industrial chains in manufacturing industry. The conversion of raw
textile fibre to finished fabric and final product draws on labour, energy, water
and other resources and cumulatively makes for a high-impact sector. The
textile and garment manufacturing industry in general is recognized as both a
major user of water and a major polluter,[1] scoring worse than any other on the
UK Environment Agency's pollution risk assessment.[2] Further, it is linked to
a litany of labour abuses including poverty wages, excessive working hours,
forced overtime, lack of job security and denial of trade union rights.[3] Yet it
also brings positive benefits, not least because it creates products that are at

the heart of our culture, and it generates wealth and employment – as many as 26 million jobs worldwide.

Designing sustainable fashion and textiles requires that we know about and support more sustainable systems of production. The issues are complex and there is no silver bullet that resolves them and provides a simple check-list of production choices for the perfect garment. Instead improvements are hard-won and come from a combination of creativity, mindfulness, information about the processes we are dealing with and an ability to adopt a life-cycle approach to affecting change. This chapter starts where the previous one left off – with raw fibre – and follows its conversion process to final product. It reviews the key environmental and social impacts of the production phase of the lifecycle and highlights opportunities to bring more sustainable improvements. This chapter explores two starting points for bringing more sustainable change in production. The first is concerned with improving individual production processes by, for example, minimizing energy and resource use and waste – the most common approach in the sector to date. The second is concerned with whole systems improvement and looks for opportunities to transform the sustainability of the underlying industrial system of which the individual processes are a part.

This chapter is organized into two parts to reflect these two starting points. The first part is focused on process improvement and is designed as a reference guide to sustainability issues and opportunities in the key processing stages. It describes efficiency measures, toxic chemical substitution and best practice in terms of baseline labour and chemical standards. The information included is technical and specific and has especial relevance to those who are hands-on makers and producers. It can be used as the basis from which to design more sustainable fashion and textiles and to guide the questions we ask of suppliers about their production processes. It also provides the building blocks on which many of the other design ideas covered in this book are based. The best-practice techniques described offer valuable benefits, especially in the short term and to the company whose process is being improved. They can lead to more efficient resource use, better relationships with workers, lower costs and valuable evidence of Corporate Social Responsibility (CSR) activity.

The second part of this chapter is concerned with systems improvements. It looks for opportunities to reduce the impact of the fashion and textile industrial system by working across the boundaries of individual processes or producers. It involves modelling the fashion and textile manufacturing industry as a whole system and searching for ways in which to improve the sustainability of the system at root. Some of these ways raise important and far-reaching questions about the relationship between business, industrial activity and long-term environmental and social quality, questions that are clearly tied in with the focus of this chapter – the production phase of the lifecycle – and which have the potential to transform the goals and rules of our design and production practice so that they are more closely aligned with sustainability.

Background to sustainability innovation in production

Before we delve into the detail of process improvements that make up the first part of this chapter, it is worth recognizing that these improvements are influenced by a number of economic, structural, legislative and cultural forces. The result is a nuanced and uneven spread of innovation across the sector that tends to reinforce the industrial status quo, while other types of improvements are little recognized. For example, while the value of whole systems improvement is widely recognized, it is little practised because of the highly fragmented structure of the textile processing chain, typically involving a large number of small and medium sized companies who tend to work on bringing change to processes that chiefly bring benefit to themselves. Other forces that have influenced sustainability innovation include the sector's cultural preference for technology-based improvements and, most significantly, legislation-driven change.

Technology-based innovation

One feature of production-related sustainability innovation is the prevalence of 'hard' technology-based improvements over 'soft' cultural change. For many manufacturers, being innovative means 'adding' technology to a problem, particularly when it is to try to ameliorate the negative impacts of existing technology. Favouring technological fixes over softer, behavioural and cultural ones is perhaps inevitable in an industry like textiles that since the Industrial Revolution in the 18th century has been processing materials faster and cheaper by improving technology. However, the result is a tendency to neglect the very substantial effect that behaviour has on determining a product's overall environmental impact (see Chapter 3 – Use Matters). It also overlooks the (significant) role of softer change in bringing sustainability improvements, and sidelines the contribution of non-technologists, like designers and consumers. Relying on technology to 'fix' all our problems can also have the more subtle and insidious effect of reinforcing our tendency to avoid accountability for our choices and behaviour.

There is a noteworthy exception to the dominance of technology-led innovation, namely the improvements that have been brought to working conditions in garment manufacturing through the introduction of non-technology-based codes of conduct. There are also signs, in the sector more generally, of a willingness to embrace softer types of change, although this has been slow to recognize the potential of design and is almost exclusively linked to the supply of information. CSR activities are good examples of this and another is the industry-led group AFIRM,[4] made up of ten leading European and US clothing brands, which meets with the express purpose of sharing information and ideas on sustainability issues.

Innovation driven by legislation

Legislation has had a formative influence on sustainability innovation in the fashion and textile sector to date. Legislation influences market forces because non-compliance is expensive and increases business risk. Businesses do 'what they can get away with', particularly when prices are low, rarely innovating beyond the minimum required in order to satisfy legal requirements. The effect is to promote a reactive and compliance-driven agenda for innovation in which environmental and social standards are perceived as a cost and a business threat and not as an opportunity. The result is that legal boundaries and pressure from consumers, non-governmental organizations (NGOs) and the media act as important mechanisms for controlling production in a market-based economy. Examples of this are: the NGO campaigns in the 1990s that exposed labour abuses in the supply chains of major brands like Nike and Gap, leading eventually to the introduction of codes of conduct setting out minimum levels of workers' rights; and legislation-driven change – again in the 1990s – that banned the use in Europe of 22 azo dyes that break down into carcinogenic amines,[5] and helped spur a more proactive approach to toxicological and pollution issues in the use of dyes.

The legislative framework itself is changing and continues to have a big effect on innovation. Until 2003, European industry's experience of pollution regulation was mainly limited to consent for discharges to sewer, but now the European Commission (EC) Integrated Pollution Prevention and Control (IPPC) regime requires companies to also make significant improvements upstream, changing their processing to reduce and even prevent impact. These improvements, or best available techniques (BAT), for the production phase of the lifecycle have been set out in a mammoth 586-page reference document.[6] The BAT range from advice to seek collaboration and information exchange on the type and load of chemicals used by upstream partners in order to create 'a chain of environmental responsibility for textiles', to measures for improving chemicals use and optimizing water consumption. Yet while the IPPC offers an important step forward it focuses almost exclusively on the sector's wet processes and its chemical use, and therefore seems to emphasize a process-improvement agenda, stopping short of introducing a fully integrated, whole lifecycle-based legal framework.

The use of chemicals in textile production falls under the EC's ambitious new programme for Registration, Evaluation and Authorisation of Chemicals (REACH) (on the statute book from 1 June 2007), which is designed to improve the current legislation on chemical substances and regulate their manufacture, import, marketing and end use.[7] REACH is a significant compliance challenge for the textile sector – as it requires safety data to be gathered about all chemicals – with major strategic business implications that could promote improved transparency of chemicals use and innovation of more environmentally benign alternatives.

More recently, however, legislation has begun to be eclipsed as the key driving force for innovation in the sector. The power to bring change has started to shift from governments to large corporations eager to protect the reputation of their brands. This shift has been given momentum by consumer and shareholder pressure on companies, motivated by greater interest in socially responsible investment and catalysed by indices of ethical performance such as the Dow Jones Sustainability Index and FTSE4Good. Company initiatives, embraced under CSR programmes, are, 'the voluntary actions that business can take, over and above compliance with minimum legal requirements, to address both its own competitive interests and the interests of wider society'.[8] Recent changes to UK law through the 2006 Companies Act now require listed companies to report on their environmental and social impacts and on employee and supplier issues, although it falls short of setting out a statutory standard for reporting.[9] Throughout the fashion and textile industry, CSR practices are increasingly recognized and supported by governments, NGOs, retailers and manufacturers and have become a major part – and even a prerequisite – of being in business. In the early 1990s Levi Strauss was the first to develop 'terms of engagement' to raise labour standards in its supply chain; more recently, Marks and Spencer and Gap Inc, for example, have placed CSR activities at the core of their business. This can be seen to represent a major shift in the way corporations respond to sustainability-related issues: moving from a strategy of compliance and risk mitigation to one of opportunistic brand differentiation. Even Topshop, owned by the Arcadia Group, which has been frequently criticized for its 'pitiful' stance on ethical issues and has been without a CSR programme until early 2007, has recently published its social and environmental strategy, following (in its words) 'an intensive period of internal review and an assessment of our current position'.[10] CSR activities go some way to countering the charges of the No Logo debate,[11] in which international companies – especially those enjoying high brand recognition – were linked to exploitation, environmental destruction, human rights abuses, disowning their domestic workforces and driving down wages.

Best practice in fibre and fabric processing

The improved processing techniques that have emerged from a mix of legislative and corporate drivers, and influenced by industry's fragmented structure and preference for technological solutions, are as multi-stage and complex as the textile industry itself (see Figure 2.1) and are reviewed in the following section. Where possible, 'best practice', that is, the processing choice that causes least impact, involves preventing impacts from arising in the first place. Yet not all processes or chemicals treatments can be avoided; indeed many are essential to producing useful and usable fashion and textile products. For essential processes, environmental impact can be reduced by emphasizing principles of minimization and optimization and by following simple guides including:

-   minimizing the number of processing steps (e.g. merge three processing stages: desizing, scouring and bleaching into a single process);
-   choosing 'clean' production techniques (e.g. reuse and exhaust dye baths);
-   minimizing processing consumables (e.g. introduce automated dosing and dispensing systems for chemicals);
-   choosing 'clean' processing chemicals (e.g. select chemicals based on minimizing overall lifecycle risk);
-   reducing energy and water consumption;
-   reducing waste production and carefully managing waste streams.

The key *environmental* challenges for the production sector are well recognized and include reducing energy, water and toxic chemical use, and minimizing the release of chemicals in wastewater. Over recent years, extensive research has been commissioned into these challenges, such as that conducted by the EC as part of its IPPC regulation. The EC sees the following processes to be of key concern:[12]

- Scouring processes prior to colouring and finishing where auxiliaries, which can be hard to biodegrade and contain hazardous compounds such as biocides, are removed.
- Desizing of cotton fabrics, which produces an effluent with high pollution index.
- Sodium hypochlorite bleaching, which gives rise to secondary reactions that form toxic organic halogen compounds.
- Hydrogen peroxide bleaching where strong complexing agents (stablizers) are used.
- Dyeing (in general) where water-polluting substances include toxic chemicals, heavy metals, alkali, salt, reducing agents, etc.
- Batch dyeing, which is inefficient and results in spent dye baths with high concentration levels.
- Printing (in general), which includes emissions to water from print paste residues and cleaning operations, and emission to air (in the form of volatile organic compounds) from drying and fixing.

The key *social* challenges are to protect workers, provide more secure employment, pay living wages, and respect workers' rights to freedom of association. These challenges lie mainly in the cut-make-trim processing stage, where labour is employed most intensively. The following section reviews the production phase of the lifecycle: the processes, their impacts and the best practice techniques to reduce these impacts.

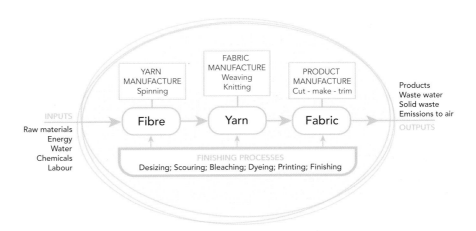

Figure 2.1 *Map of key processes, inputs and outputs in the textile production chain*

Spinning, weaving and knitting

Spinning, weaving and knitting are largely mechanical processes and the major environmental burdens are related to energy use, solid waste production and the generation of dust and noise. In addition all three processes involve the application of lubricants (in spinning), oils (in knitting) or size (in weaving) to strengthen and protect the fibres from the stresses of processing. These coatings and lubricants become waste as they are washed out of the fabric prior to dyeing (in scouring) and can be hard to treat, as they are slow to biodegrade.

Overall the environmental impact of weaving is higher than that of knitting, because of the use of size. Sizing agents are applied to the warp to prevent thread breakage during weaving and need to be completely removed before further processing. This is done in the desizing step, often with a large amount of water and the addition of process chemicals. The resulting effluent is highly polluting and while some sizing agents can be reclaimed and reused from the desizing liquor (like polyvinyl alcohol (PVA)), which has the potential to cut pollution load by a massive 94 per cent,[13] more often cheap, natural starches are used that are impossible to recover and have to be neutralized in the effluent treatment plant. This is because weaving and fabric finishing are normally separate activities, carried out by different companies, frequently in different countries, and there is little financial incentive for weavers to use more expensive synthetic sizes when it is a downstream producer who enjoys the benefits. In addition to sizing agents any biocides, like pentachlorophenols (PCPs), a rot-proofing agent, added to cotton fabric to protect it in storage and transport, are washed out in desizing. Emission of these substances is outlawed in the EU and the US for their negative effects on nervous, reproductive and renal systems and for their carcinogenic properties.

Best practice in yarn and fabric manufacture includes the following:[14]

- In spinning, ask suppliers to manufacture yarn with readily biodegradable lubricants.
- In knitting, ask suppliers to use water soluble and biodegradable lubricants as substitutes for mineral oils.
- Avoid woven fabrics where PCPs have been added as a size preservative.
- Ask suppliers to substitute recyclable sizing agents for natural starches and use 'low add-on techniques' that minimize the amount of size used.
- If recyclable sizing agents are used, check with suppliers that size is recovered and reused.

- If unknown sizing agents are used, check with suppliers that size is removed with efficient techniques such as the oxidative route[15] and ensure adequate effluent treatment.
- Ask suppliers to combine scouring and desizing processes with bleaching to save chemicals, energy and water.

Impact can also be reduced through the introduction of innovative production technology such as whole garment or seamless knitting. Whole garment knit-wear is made in one entire piece, three-dimensionally directly on the knitting machine and is reported to have significant energy saving potential – it takes around 30 to 40 per cent less time than for conventional sew and manufacture.[16] In addition, whole garment technologies reduce labour costs (there are no post-production labour costs), lead-times (by allowing on-demand production) and eliminate fabric waste or cut-loss.[17]

Fabric finishing

The final stage in fabric processing is known as finishing and includes preparation of the fabric to be dyed and/or printed, dyeing and printing itself and the application of any specialist fabric finishes such as those giving water repellency and crease resistance. Finishing is the chief cause of environmental impacts in the production phase, using significant quantities of water, energy and chemicals and producing substantial amounts of effluent. Some of the chemicals used contain toxics, such as heavy metals like copper, chromium and cobalt, which are known carcinogens, dioxins – also carcinogenic and suspected hormone disrupters – and formaldehyde, a suspected carcinogen. Effluents from the textile processing chain are characterized by their grey colour, high polluting load, high solids content and high temperature.[18] To avoid breaching pollution regulations, effluents have to be treated prior to discharge. A standard sequence of effluent treatment for woven or knit fabric finishing includes: screening, to remove fibrous waste from the effluent; equalization, to mix waste in order to achieve a fairly standard effluent for downstream processing; and biological treatment, to lower the effluent's polluting load. In biological treatment, micro-organisms are grown to feed on the substrates in the effluent and require a treatment time of between 24 and 48 hours. However, some pollutants are untreatable and for these, prevention, not treatment, is the primary concern. Such a preventative approach can be seen in the Soil Association's organic textile standards,[19] for instance, which does not allow the use of certain process chemicals in its accredited products (including, among others, aromatic or halogenated solvents, PCPs, formaldehyde, heavy metals except for iron and 5 per cent copper in blue-green dyestuffs) and allows others to be used only in closely monitored processes, such as ammonia pre-treatments for wool in a closed circuit. Prevention is also built-in to the Climatex Lifecycle range of furnishing fabrics,[20] designed to biodegrade completely and safely at the end of their life. In order to avoid the release into the environment of any carcinogens, persistent toxic chemicals, heavy metals or other toxic substances, Climatex Lifecycle is processed coloured only with carefully selected chemicals (out of over 8000 chemicals used in the textile industry, only 38 were deemed suitable), that provide no biological or ecological hazard as the fabric breaks down.

Bleaching

Most natural fibres have an off-white colour, so bleaching is necessary to produce white fabrics and those that will be dyed or printed to pale colours. Manufactured fibres are also bleached as it enhances colour brilliance after dyeing, improves colour uniformity – even for dark shades – and removes the last traces of residual impurities. Bleaching does, however, undermine fibre strength and thus the durability of the textile product. The oldest known method of fabric bleaching is sun bleaching, requiring around 36 hours of direct sunlight to break down coloured molecules and lighten a fabric.

Today in Europe, it is common practice to bleach with hydrogen peroxide in a wet process. Hydrogen peroxide is active only at temperatures above 60°C, resulting in a fairly energy-intensive bleaching process. Chemical additives are needed in the bleaching bath to stabilize the hydrogen peroxide and optimize the bleaching process, giving a fabric with uniform appearance. One of these additives (sequestering agents) counters the effect of reactive metal particles present in the bath that otherwise would act as a catalyst for the bleaching agent and cause it to attack and breakdown the fibre. Sequestering agents, if discharged untreated, are considered to be highly polluting.

Fibres can also be bleached with chlorine-based products like sodium hypochlorite and sodium chlorite; however, concerns about the negative effects of these products on the reproductive and immune system have meant that chlorine is no longer seen as an acceptable bleaching agent. Indeed there are now strategies in place for the phase-out of chlorine in manufacturing more generally. Although for some fibres, like hemp, white fabrics can be produced only by bleaching with chlorine and here a two-stage process, first using hydrogen peroxide and then sodium chlorite, is recommended to reduce impact.

Best practice in bleaching:[21]

- Ask suppliers to combine bleaching with scouring (and desizing if appropriate) to save chemicals, energy and water.
- Use hydrogen peroxide as the preferred bleaching agent combined with techniques to minimize the use of stabilizers.
- Check that suppliers biologically treat wastewater prior to discharge.

Dyeing

Textiles can be dyed as fibres, yarn or fabric. Different fibres have an affinity for different dyes, and different colours and shades of colours use different dye classes. The dye bath contains processing (auxiliary) chemicals as well as dye. These chemicals vary by dye, dyer and machine, as does liquor ratio (the ratio of water to chemicals), water temperature and dyeing time. As a result the actual consumption of dye varies between 2 and 80g per kilogram of textile (with an average of 20g/kg) depending on depth of colour.[22] After dyeing, the yarn or fabric requires intensive washing to remove auxiliary chemicals in addition to any unfixed dye. The dyeing process is resource intensive in terms of water, energy and chemicals and produces effluent that is often highly coloured, with dyes being the most likely source of major metal pollutants (such as zinc, copper and chromium)[23] (see Table 2.1). In countries with poor working conditions and few environmental protection measures, dyeing and printing can pose a serious threat to human and environmental health. Reducing this threat is a complex task as no one dyestuff provides the best answer to low impact dyeing. Similarly, no one colour can be singled out as having the 'best' or 'worst' environmental load – although certain shades, most notably blue, green and turquoise are difficult to achieve without the use of copper (a heavy metal). In general terms, the darker the shade, the greater the amount of dye lost to effluent. Therefore some scope for improvement exists by avoiding dark, heavy shades such as navy and black. Although the environmental benefit of avoiding dyeing to dark shades may be cancelled out in laundering, as light shades tend to show the dirt more easily and so may be laundered more frequently, causing more impact in the use phase (see Chapter 3 – Use Matters). This highlights yet again one of the central challenges of sustainability for the fashion and textile sector: to simultaneously act for positive change at the large and small scales – a theme we come back to over and again in the course of this book.

Many steps have been taken to reduce the impacts of dyeing processes, particularly in response to legal restrictions on pollution, most notably

Table 2.1 *Types of pollution associated with dyeing a range of fibres*[24]
Note: *Categories of pollution are as follows: 1 = relatively harmless; 2 = readily biodegradable; 3 = difficult to biodegrade; 4 = difficult to biodegrade, moderate pollution load; 5 = unsuitable for conventional biological treatment.*

Fibre	Dye class	Percentage of non-fixed dye that may be discharged	Type of pollution
Cotton	Directs	30%	1 salt 3 unfixed dye 5 copper salts, cationic fixing agents
	Reactives	50%	1 salt, alkali 3 unfixed dye
	Vats	25%	1 alkali, oxidizing agents 2 reducing agents
	Sulphurs	25%	1 alkali, oxidizing agents 2 reducing agents 3 unfixed dye
Wool	Chromes	1-2%	2 organic acids 5 heavy metal salts
	1:2 metal complexes	10%	2 organic acids
	Acids	10%	2 organic acids 3 unfixed dye
Polyester	Disperse	15%	2 reducing agents, organic acids 5 carriers

contaminated effluent, and on the use of toxic chemicals. While there have been some advances in the chemical make-up of dyes and pigments themselves, the most effective action has come from technological developments in dyeing techniques. For example, techniques to recover, reuse and 'exhaust' dye baths is proving effective in reducing both volumes of effluent and the use of chemicals. Dye bath reuse has already been applied while disperse dyeing polyester, reactive dyeing cotton, acid dyeing nylon and basic dyeing acrylic, on a wide variety of machines. The likelihood of dye liquor reuse is increased especially when dyeing is limited to a few shades – like in nylon hosiery – where given the right conditions a dye liquor could be reused up to ten times before the level of impurities limits further use.

Table 2.2 *Summary of developments in dye chemistry*[25]

Dye	Key challenges to be overcome	Best Practice
Reactive dyes	Poor dye fixation, which in the worst case can lead to up to 50% of the dye unfixed and high salt concentrations to fix the dye to the fibre	Bi-functional and low-salt reactive dyes that can give greater than 95% fixation Follow dyeing by a hot rinsing process, which can avoid the use of detergents and complexing agents in the neutralization step
Sulphur dyes	Use of sodium sulphide to 'reduce' dye so that it penetrates the fibre	Stabilized non-pre-reduced sulphide-free dyes Replace sodium sulphide with sulphur-free reducing agent
Chrome dyes for wool	Use of chrome – a highly polluting heavy metal	Substitute chrome dyes for reactive dyes. Where not possible use ultra-low chroming methods
Metal complex dyes for wool	Discharge of heavy metals in the waste water	Use auxiliaries to enhance dye uptake and pH-control methods to exhaust dye bath
Acid and basic dyes for wool	Use of organic levelling agents	Use pH-controlled process to maximize dye exhaustion and minimize use of organic levelling agents
Disperse dyes for polyester	Use of hazardous carriers and non-biodegradable dispersing agents	Avoid the use of carriers by using a modified non-carrier dyeable polyester Dye in high temperature conditions without the use of carriers Use dispersing agents with a high degree of bioeliminability

Another example of improved dyeing techniques is pad-batch dyeing, suitable for cellulosic fibres like cotton, linen and viscose, and which saves energy, water, dyes, chemicals, labour and floor space.[26] The technique involves steeping the fabric in dye liquor, 'batching' it into rolls, covering it with plastic film and storing for up to 12 hours, after which it is washed. In addition, other improved dyeing techniques include: electrochemical dyeing, where an electric current enables a spent dye bath to be regenerated and the dye recycled;[27] and the possibility of dyeing with non-aqueous systems, either with super-critical carbon dioxide or ionic liquids in place of water in the dye bath. While originally these systems were only suitable for dyeing hydrophobic fibres like polyester and nylon, more recently combinations of dyes have been specifically designed to colour natural fibres.[28] Innovations in dye chemistry comprise work on the development of disperse dyes as 'universal dyes' suitable for dyeing all fibre types, which would reduce both the complexity of the dyeing process and the waste streams,[28] and a range of improvements in most dye groups, as summarized in Table 2.2.

Natural dyes, made from plants, animals and shells provide important alternatives to petrochemical-based dyes and, if harvesting is carefully managed, offer environmental and social benefits including a low carbon footprint and valuable employment for rural communities. They are not without disadvantages, however, predominantly linked to the dependency of natural dye processes on chemicals to fix the dye to the fabric and the difficulty of using natural dyes on an industrial scale. The five classic dyestuffs are madder, cochineal, weld, cutch and indigo, which give a good range of colours, although there are many other sources including nettles, rhubarb root and walnut hulls. Natural dyes are suitable for colouring natural fibres only and in the majority of cases have no built-in affiliation for the fibre and so fixing agents (mordants) are required. Mordants are commonly, though not exclusively, polluting heavy metals (including chromium and tin), although other alternatives exist, such as oak galls, yeast and urine. In comparison to synthetic dyes, natural dyes have large variations in colour tone, because of the quality differences of different provenances of the dye plant, which can make colour matching difficult; they require longer, slower dyeing treatments to achieve good colour, particularly for vegetable fibres – making the process more costly than dyeing with synthetics; and they also require large quantities of materials for small amounts of dye, as concentrations of dye found in nature tend to be extremely low. Yet their higher cost, subtle colour variation and greater demands on time means that natural dye technology – as it stands today – has a particular cachet and quality that works well in small-scale or specialist production. Scaling natural dye processes up to become acceptable to industry will require sustained research and development to address such difficulties as the water-insoluble natural dye material (normally in a powdered or chopped form), which is much less easy to use than solid and water-soluble synthetic dyes. That difficulty has been overcome in part by providing dyers with watery extracts of dye instead of large dye bags full of natural material.[30]

Best practice in dyeing:[31]

- Use automated systems for dosing and dispensing chemicals and controlling machine variables, to maximize efficiency.
- Check that suppliers have introduced water and energy efficiency measures.
- Ask suppliers to guarantee low liquor dyeing and associated improved dye fixation.

- Avoid fabrics dyed with hazardous dyestuffs and auxiliaries; substituting alternatives that are biodegradable or bio-eliminable.
- Ask suppliers to reuse and exhaust dye liquors on repeat shades and reuse rinse water for the next dyeing.
- Check that wastewater is treated prior to discharge.

Printing

Printing is one of the most chemically complex areas in textile processing. It is possible to print with almost all classes of dye needing a wide range of chemical auxiliaries. Textile printing involves the accurate application of a colour paste, made up of dye or pigment, a thickening agent and other chemicals, onto a fabric. Unlike in dyeing, colour is applied to specific, selected areas of fabric, which reduces resource consumption. There are many different methods of printing, such as flat screen, roller, transfer and ink jet, each with different demands on resources. In screen printing for example, impact can be reduced by reducing print paste losses in machine pipes and squeegees and with careful cleaning of screens and belts with reused rinsing water and by switching to water-based PVC- and phthalate-free printing formulations (now widely available) that do not contain aromatic solvents, which are harmful to watercourses on discharge. Digital printing, the most popular form of which uses ink jets, involves the propelling of tiny droplets of dye or pigment onto a fabric electrostatically. In ink-jet printing, the selected dyes or pigments are dosed on demand and avoid print paste residues at the end of each run, and if pigmented inks are used (rather than those based on dyes) no solvent, with associated volatile organic compound emissions, is required to dissolve the colourant. Further, pigment-based inks can be cured with novel ultra-violet curing technology, where UV radiation is used to rapidly fix the printing ink to the fabric without the emission of odour or toxic by-products, offering advantages over traditional methods of drying by heating and steaming.[32]

Of particular note is transfer printing, which has important advantages in comparison to other methods of printing. In transfer printing, paper is first printed with volatile disperse dyes and then heated, together with the fabric, in a thermapress. Under these conditions the dyestuff is transferred from the paper to the textile material by sublimation. In transfer printing only the dyestuff and no other chemical is deposited on the fabric, so no washing-off is required and no effluent generated. For conventional printing 250kg of water per kilogram of printed fabric is required; for transfer printing, only 2kg is needed.[33] In its present form transfer printing is only suitable for some synthetic fibres and is particularly successful with polyester.

Best practice in printing:[34]

- Choose suppliers who use water-based print formulations.
- Ask suppliers about measures to reduce print paste losses and water consumption in screen printing.
- Use digital ink-jet printing for short production runs to reduce print paste waste.
- Choose suppliers who substitute the use of urea in reactive printing by introducing novel printing methods.
- In pigment printing ask suppliers to use thickeners which contain no volatile solvents, to minimize emissions to air as print pastes are dried.

Specialist fabric finishing

Textiles can be given a range of additional treatments after dyeing and printing, to improve either fabric performance or aesthetics. Some treatments are mechanical, such as calendering, where the fabric is pressed between rollers, giving it a glaze and increasing its density. Others are chemical, such as those providing water repellency and crease resistance (easy-care). Making cellulosic fabrics easy-care has traditionally involved a treatment of urea and formaldehyde that when baked onto the fabric forms a resinous polymer and makes the fabric less prone to creasing. The use of formaldehyde is now restricted; it is a skin irritant and is linked to the production of carcinogens. As a result formaldehyde-free or formaldehyde-poor techniques have been developed. Other treatments give water repellency. Traditional treatments made use of paraffin wax coatings that need regular reapplication to maintain water tightness. More durable finishes that withstand washing and repel oily stains as well as water are based on perfluorinated chemicals, which have wide ranging health impacts and are persistent in the environment. Recently the UK Government has announced plans to phase out one widely used perfluorinated chemical (PFOS) and 3M, maker of Scotchguard, the stain-resistant coating for textiles, has withdrawn from 'perfluoroctanyl chemistry' because of risks to human health. In the near future Europe seems likely to regulate against non-essential uses of perfluorocarbons, including in stain-repellent coatings on fabrics, which account for substantial use of the chemicals, yet deliver few benefits.[35]

Other finishes still provide antimicrobial protection, either with organochlorines such as triclosan, the primary ingredient of the registered biocide Microban (suitable for polyester and nylon fibres and their blends with cotton and wool), or with coatings such as poly(hexamethylenebiguanide) (suitable for cellulosic fibres). While the side effects of these bacteria-killing coatings are still largely unknown, there is growing unease about the possibility that their widespread use might result in bacteria (so-called super bugs) developing resistance to drugs with the same mode of action.[36] All specialist finishes are applied to add value to the final product, where they can, for example, lead to reduced impacts in washing or enhanced product durability. The remaining largely untested question is whether these benefits outweigh the negative impacts in the processing stage and whether adding more and more complex treatments in production reduces the textile's overall lifecycle impact.

Best practice in specialist fabric finishing:[37]

- Ask for formaldehyde-free or formaldehyde-poor easy-care finishing agents.
- Minimize energy consumption of drying machines (stenters).
- Use recipes optimized for low air emissions.

Cut-make-trim

Following fabric finishing, cloth is cut and sewn into garments or other textile products. The cut-make-trim (CMT) stage is a largely manual operation – with key sustainability impacts being social and worker related rather than environmental, in sharp contrast to the finishing stage. Converting pattern pieces to garments needs workers at sewing machines – an inexpensive, mechanically simple technology. This results in a 'mobile' industry that is relocated to whichever area of the globe has the cheapest labour costs. Manufacturers compete with each other for a place in the supply chain of retailers and big brands and this puts downward pressure on labour rights and working conditions, making these the key impacts associated with garment manufacture.[38] This downward pressure has increased, according to Fashioning an Ethical Industry, a project of the campaigning group Labour Behind the Label, with the removal of trade protection barriers in the textile and garment sector on 1 January 2005:

> In order to remain competitive, governments and employers feel the need to offer the cheapest, most flexible labour in the least regulated workplace. This translates into downgrading working conditions and wages and stepping up trade union repression. Lesotho, El Salvador and Sri Lanka for instance have excluded textile and garment workers from

statutory wage increases; Bangladesh for a while legalised a 72 hour working week; in the Philippines, unpaid overtime is becoming the norm. Flexibilisation translates into informalisation, which means reduced legal production for workers.[39]

Evidence for labour abuses in the supply chains of high street names is convincing. War on Want's recent report, *Fashion Victims,* for example, revealed that Bangladeshi workers making goods for UK retailers are working 80-hour weeks for 5p an hour despite pledges by these companies to protect basic human rights.[40] Oxfam's report *Offside!*, published to coincide with the 2006 Football World Cup, revealed the serious labour abuses in the supply chains of many global sports brands, including workers being dismissed or threatened with violence when they have organized unions to lobby for better pay and conditions.[41] In another report, Labour Behind the Label shed light on the 'poverty wages' paid to many working in the garment sector. Here commitments of retailers and big brands to pay workers minimum wages are undermined because neither national legal standards nor industry benchmark standards come close to meeting basic needs. In Bangladesh, for example, the minimum wage is £7 per week whereas the living wage is calculated as £30 per week.[42] Low pay, lack of rights and unacceptable working conditions is the daily reality for millions of garment workers across the world – conditions that are tolerated because workers need an income – and working in poor conditions in the clothing supply chain is perhaps better than some of the alternatives available, particularly for low-skilled female workers.

Codes of conduct

Since violations of workers' rights were first brought to public attention in the 1990s, there has been growing pressure from the public, trade unions and campaigning groups to improve labour rights and working conditions in the textile and clothing sector. Ethical trade initiatives have succeeded most by helping retailers and brands acknowledge their responsibility to the workers in their supply chains, mainly through the development of codes of conduct. Codes of conduct outline basic workers' rights and minimum standards pledged by a company and can help raise awareness, put pressure on fashion companies and factories to meet basic standards and provide guidance for law making. Codes are voluntary agreements, frequently drawn up by the company themselves, and are passed onto contracted factories to sign. Consequently, codes vary enormously and this has led NGOs and trade unions to develop 'model' codes that include details of proper monitoring and independent verification procedures. Monitoring and verification is vital to ensure the code is more than just a list of good intentions and is implemented in an effective and systematic way.

The Clean Clothes Campaign[43] has developed one such model code, building on international standards. It states that:

-    employment is freely chosen;
-    there is no discrimination in employment;
-    child labour is not used;
-    freedom of association and the right to collective bargaining are respected;
-    living wages are paid;
-    hours of work are not excessive;
-    working conditions are decent;
-    the employment relationship is established.

The most progressive codes of conduct are developed in collaboration with workers, trade unions and NGOs in a bottom-up approach called a 'multi-stakeholder initiative'; the most stringent of these is that developed by Social Accountability International and its SA 8000 Standard.[44] These initiatives emphasize worker education and training, the right to form a union and the active involvement of workers, local NGOs and independent auditors in the monitoring of standards. This helps prevent codes bringing only temporary change to the lives of workers – such as around the time a contract is signed for instance, or during occasional, pre-organized monitoring visits. Major violations of workers' rights, for example, have been recorded in factories that have passed social audits. Indeed even with extensive implementation, monitoring and verification procedures, such as those put in place by the most forward-looking multinational corporations, problems still exist; Nike, for example, admits that even with strict codes and independent monitoring, up to half of its workers do not even receive the legal minimum wage.[45] To make change happen will therefore take more than a code – a point recognized by forums such as the Ethical Trading Initiative,[46] which provides corporate members with a safe space for discussion with other companies and for engagement with critical NGOs and trade unions. It conducts pilot projects and has set up a number of working groups to look into various aspects of code implementation.

Modelling the industry as a whole system

In the first part of this chapter we saw how more efficient processing techniques and codes of conduct can help reduce the negative impacts of the way business is done in the fashion and textile sector. These codes and techniques have evolved out of the economic and technological reality of production conditions in today's industry. They play a vital role in bringing tangible and sometimes instant environmental benefits and act as an important driving force in getting retailers to take more responsibility for the workers in their supply chains.

The next part of this chapter changes in emphasis and switches away from a close focus on process improvement to a systems view of sustainability improvements across the industry as a whole. It does this by interweaving culture, behaviour and industrial activity to help contextualize the standards- and process-driven improvements in a bigger picture of possible and more sustainable actions. This 'bigger picture' involves us moving from a reductionist approach to tackling sustainability issues (i.e. looking at individual issues, materials, methods and companies) to a whole industry-as-system approach. When we consider the fashion and textile industry as a system, new and different opportunities for bringing more sustainable change are revealed. This change happens at many levels, some with more far-reaching influence than others.

Donella Meadows,[47] an inspirational and visionary complex systems theorist, has developed a list of systems intervention or leverage points each with greater influence than the last. The next part of this chapter explores this list using case studies from the fashion and textile sector. It draws on a growing band of designer-makers, large companies and collaborative projects that are working towards change in different ways and can be described as 'intervening' at different points in the fashion and textile industrial system. They are producing products and championing approaches that support communities and respect workers; that promote information and supply chain transparency; and that offer us more effective, imaginative and conscientious models of production. These projects and companies are both high end and high street and comprise a wealth of different production configurations, ranging from one-off craft or bespoke production; to networks of small suppliers, normally organized into co-operatives; to vertically integrated manufacturing; to manufacturing on multiple sites with strict codes of conduct and supply chain standards. Donella Meadows' list helps explain why certain types of change bring short-term benefits and why others have deeper, broader and longer-lasting effects. It also builds confidence and shows us how our actions (including small actions) can affect the bigger system. Meadows lists nine 'places to intervene in a system', which are a set of tactics, of varying effectiveness, for changing current practices. From least to the most effective, they are:

9   numbers (subsidies, taxes, standards);

8   material stocks and flows;

7   regulating negative feedback loops;

6   driving positive feedback loops;

5   information flows;

4   the rules of the system (incentives, punishment, constraints);

3   the power of self-organization;

2   the goals of the system;

1   the mindset or paradigm out of which the goals, rules, feedback structure arise.

9 Numbers and standards

For Donella Meadows, a focus on standards or efficiency targets tends to bring the most limited change because it involves only minor adjustments to a product or process. Adjusting numbers and standards may change efficiency ratings, but because these improved ratings are being applied to the same fibres, processed with the same machinery, sold by the same retailers as before, the system does not change much. So for example, if we filter wastewater, it cuts down on river pollution downstream from the dyehouse, but it does not make a dye process low-impact. Likewise, if retailers introduce recyclable packaging, it positively reduces the amount of waste sent to landfill, but it does not tackle problems linked to over-design of packaging and over-consumption of resources more generally.

Yet numbers and standards is where most change tends to start (and where the vast majority of sustainability actions of the fashion and textiles sector have been concentrated to date) because it tends to be in the direct influence of most companies. These manufacturers can, for example, fine-tune an inefficient process far quicker and easier than they can redesign the overall system. Yet Meadows' point is that it is important not to focus on making changes only at this level (many of us seem to get 'stuck' here) because while the benefits tend to be felt quite quickly and are particularly important for the company whose process is being improved, they will not on their own completely transform the sector into a more sustainable one. To achieve sustainability, we need to develop other tactics too and use the focus on numbers and standards as the start of a process of questioning, thinking and improving to drive fundamentally deeper and longer-term change.

8 Material stocks and flows

Substituting one material for another and introducing innovative products can have an enormous effect on how a system operates, particularly in a manufacturing-led industry like fashion and textiles. A key way to support more sustainable material flows in our industry is to build large, stable material stocks of, say, low-impact fibres. This will help ensure that the lower impact alternatives are widely available and readily taken up. To increase the stocks of these fibres, suppliers need to be drawn into the market. To make this happen, there needs to be strong, dependable demand. Guaranteed markets for fibres like organic cotton protect farmers from price fluctuations in commodity markets; and for recycled fibres like polyester or wool, encourage research and development in the building of successful new markets for second-hand materials.

Retailer Marks and Spencer[48] (M&S), which accounts for around 10 per cent of the UK's clothing market, is successfully influencing stock and flow structures. For over a decade, M&S has been working to reduce the impact of its own-brand products, mainly through the introduction of strict production standards across the supply chain that, for example, banned suppliers from using certain dye chemicals and insisted on the removal of all other dyes before the effluent is released to the environment (these follow many of the best practice guidance set out in the first part of this chapter). More recently its focus on standards and material flows has been transformed: first, in 2006, as it launched a major advertising campaign (Look Behind the Label) to differentiate its brand on the basis of its CSR policies, including care over the chemicals used in its products; and then in 2007, with the launch of its progressive 100-point sustainability initiative, 'Plan A'. Plan A commits M&S, by 2012, to become carbon-neutral, to send no waste to landfill and, most ambitiously, to extend sustainable sourcing and set new standards in ethical trading. In its sourcing policy, it has pledged to launch product lines in organic cotton, linen and wool and use recycled polyester. It is also committed to Fair Trade cotton. Its estimate is that by 2008 20 million of its garments will carry the Fairtrade mark for cotton – an independent product certification label that guarantees sweat-free cotton farming and a minimum price for the crop. It is the sheer size of M&S's operation – its influence extends to over 2000 factories, 10,000 farms, 250,000 workers and millions of customers – that makes acting to build a strong market in more sustainable materials a powerful way to effect change of the bigger system.

▶ T-shirts in 100 per cent Fairtrade mark cotton by Marks and Spencer

7 Regulating negative feedback loops

Negative feedback loops help maintain systems within safe limits. They focus on keeping undesirable factors under control by looking at the output of the system and reducing it (hence the term 'negative') to keep the system in check (see Figure 2.2). In the case of the fashion and textile sector these impact-reducing loops are provided by legislation or pressure from consumers and NGOs. Rafts of new European legislation including IPPC, REACH and producer responsibility 'take back' legislation – which requires companies to take their products back from consumers at the end of their lives (already on the statute book for electronic products and likely to be extended to other sectors) – are all negative feedback loops and act to reduce the impact of industry. Other examples include codes of conduct, effectively lobbied for by a number of campaigning groups including Labour Behind the Label and Oxfam, which have acted to promote workers' rights by controlling the amount of overtime worked and by safeguarding pay, working conditions and the right to join a union.

Yet negative feedback loops are only effective if they are as strong as the impacts they are trying to keep in check. New business pressures such as the push to supply 'value' clothes and reduce lead times are ratcheting up the level of impact. In the last five years, for example, the lead times expected by big retailers and global brands from their suppliers have been cut by 30 per cent.[49] This prevents long-term planning by supplier factories and fuels a cycle of lowering labour standards as workers are forced into unpaid overtime to meet deadlines, frequently on temporary contracts. This has resulted in a 'race to the bottom' in terms of labour standards and prices as countries

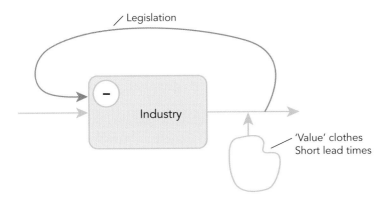

Figure 2.2 *Negative feedback loop*

compete for contracts from leading brands and retailers, and an increased level of 'throwaway' consumption – the average UK consumer today buys up to one third more textiles and garments than four years ago.[50] To continue to be effective and keep impacts in check, the strength of codes and regulations will have to increase (with ever more prescriptive legislation) unless we address issues to do with consumption and relationships between brands and suppliers in other ways.

6 Driving positive feedback loops

A number of fashion and textiles companies and projects are pushing for change using positive feedback loops. These loops are powerful and self-reinforcing and can drive growth with important effects on the bigger system (see Figure 2.3). There is, for example, a loop of positive feedback around encouraging the growth of sustainable fashion. The more consumer interest there is in environmental and social issues, the more products will be offered by fashion companies keen to have a share of the market. This increased choice and raised profile leads to more consumer interest in the issues and greater demand for sustainable products. And so the loop goes on, positively reinforcing this market.

EDUN, the clothing brand set up by Ali Hewson, wife of rock star Bono, uses positive feedback loops to effect change. EDUN focuses on poverty reduction through trade and sustainable employment, especially in Africa. One of its recent campaigns 'One'[51] focuses on supporting the precarious clothing industry in Lesotho through a combination of trade and aid. The removal of global import quotas in the textile sector in 2005 left a number of countries – such as Lesotho – that built great dependency on the textile and

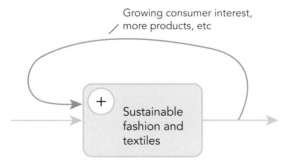

Growing consumer interest, more products, etc

Sustainable fashion and textiles

Figure 2.3 *Positive feedback loop*

◄ ONE T-shirt made from 100 per cent Lesotho cotton by EDUN

clothing industry in the era of quotas, at risk of widespread economic hardship. In Lesotho, for instance, the clothing sector accounts for around 40 per cent of national jobs. The positive feedback loop is established by providing factories in Lesotho with guaranteed work, which then creates more jobs and raises more people out of poverty, which in turn increases Lesotho's industry and capacity to work. Further, a quarter of the ticket price of EDUN's Lesotho-made One T-shirts is ploughed back into AIDS prevention and medicines for the factory workers – AIDS claiming the lives of around 2300 of Lesotho's garment workers each year.

Another positive feedback loop is created by Aid to Artisans,[52] a non-profit organization that provides 'a world community' of entrepreneur-craftspeople with access to programmes of product design, production and business skills to strengthen their businesses and ultimately to build self-reliance and support families, communities and livelihoods. Here the loop is initiated by information: the more knowledge of the market Aid to Artisans can provide an entrepreneur, the more products that are sold and the more self-reliance fostered in the community. This then leads to more knowledge and experience of the market and helps the entrepreneur grow their business. Aid to Artisans' work spans more than 140 artisan groups, helping them to create sustainable businesses. The Sharan Craft Centre (SCC) in Armenia, for example, gained design assistance from Aid to Artisans as a fledgling enterprise and is now a fully independent and thriving children's knitwear business with an annual turnover of US$600,000, employing over 400 artisans, to whom it pays an average wage over 50 per cent higher than the average national wage.

5 Information flows

Adding or changing the flows of information between companies in a supply chain or between retailers, designers and consumers can bring big change for relatively little effort – compared say to changing a company's equipment or factory set-up. The power of information in bringing more sustainable change is recognized, for example, by the EC in its IPPC recommendations, where exchanging information on the type and load of chemicals used by upstream partners in the supply chain can help create 'a chain of environmental responsibility for textiles'. Other examples include CSR programmes that use information strategically to bring change inside corporations and also with outside stakeholders; and the Made-By[53] supply chain traceability initiative for fashion brands pushes this further by introducing a new flow of

information about sustainability impacts into the fashion industry system. Using sophisticated tracking technology and an Internet interface, the Made-By initiative links up with a fashion brand to show all the production processes behind a product, including where it was made, from what and by whom and publishes the data on its website for consumers to access. Its goal is to ensure absolute transparency of the supply chain (both good and bad) with the hope that openness will lead to more responsible practices. Some garments produced under the Made-By label carry a small blue button near the care label and an identification tag that uniquely identifies a single batch of product. By entering the data on this label into the Made-By website and 'pushing the button' a full garment production history is revealed.

▲ Pillows produced by Armenian craftspeople supported by Aid to Artisans

4 The rules of the system

The system rules define the scope and boundaries of the fashion and textile industry and set out who benefits. They can for example set out new relationships with workers or a different approach to resource use. A number of companies are working at the level of rules to influence the bigger system. The business model at People Tree,[54] for example, is designed around Fair Trade and ecological principles. People Tree produces simple, pretty and natural fibre garments, some made with organic cotton, in collaboration with 70 Fair Trade groups in 20 developing countries, normally operating as cooperatives.

It pays producer partners a fair price, offering advance payment, provides technical and design assistance and commits to regular, ongoing orders with achievable lead times. Its products rely on the specialist skills of over 1400 artisans and include hand-woven cotton from Bangladesh, delicately beaded Zardosi embroidery from India and Japanese Hanga woodblock printing. Particularly in labour-intensive manufacturing stages like garment production, Fair Trade initiatives bring important benefits for workers.

The business model of American Apparel[55] – now the biggest T-shirt manufacturer in the US – also has different rules. Its multi-coloured knitted jersey sweatshirts and T-shirts are celebrated as 'Made in Downtown LA, Sweatshop Free', where it has developed a strong brand image around credibility within its organization by dedication to its workers. American Apparel has sidestepped criticism often levelled at clothing labels about their ignorance of labour and working conditions in factories in low-cost countries (out of sight, out of mind) by making all its clothes in a vertically integrated mill in its own backyard. Advertising and marketing are also in-house – with factory workers modelling in its ad campaigns. American Apparel pays above the US minimum wage and provides staff with benefits that include company-subsidized lunches, bus passes, free English language classes, on-site masseurs and free bicycles.

▶ Made-By
button
indicating
supply chain
transparency

Purple
hooded
sweatshirt and
white T-shirt
by American
Apparel

Christina Kim's high-end label Dosa[56] also intervenes at the level of rules, combining a sense of a personal responsibility for workers with environmental awareness. Kim uses traditional hand-loomed khadi fabrics, organic wool, undyed hand-spun wild silk, natural dyes such as cochineal, fustic and indigo and avoids chemical bleaches. Dosa's products frequently use hand techniques to infuse the product with a sense of the energy and touch of the maker and support rural communities – the label's demand for hand-spun silk for example, provides livelihoods for 500 women in the Assam region of India. Rewriting the rules about sales and consumption, Kim also avoids the practice of designing new collections for multiple seasons, instead producing a new collection once a year.

3 The power of self-organization

Self-organization is a process in which a system's internal organization increases in effectiveness without being guided or managed by an outside source. It happens without any controlling 'brain' and instead involves cooperative working between each part of the system, adapting as needed to help with the functioning of the whole. Providing the people in the system are armed with information, knowledge and choice, then it can lead to positive and substantial change. The best way for us to do this is to set up the ideal conditions for making this happen. In fashion and textiles this means generating the biggest stock possible of sustainability-related ideas, materials, behaviours and culture from which to seed the building of new, or more effective versions of existing, systems. To promote self-organization we have to promote diversity and build as broad a range of potential solutions and ideas as possible. This pluralistic vision, of building a multitude of diverse and engaging approaches, is at the heart of this book.

2 The goals of the system

The goals of the system profoundly influence its dynamics, impacts and products. The fashion and textile industry's whole-system goal is to make profit through selling fibres, fabrics and garments. These profits help businesses grow and control more of the market, which then reduces their exposure to financial risk. Changing these goals to promote sustainability and to balance the making of profit with social and environmental quality would lead to big change (impacting on all of the other leverage points on this list). Outdoor sportswear producer Patagonia and carpet giant Interface are both companies with transformed, sustainability-focused business goals (both of these

◀ Slip dress in
100 per cent
silk by Dosa

companies are discussed elsewhere in this book). In both cases these companies were transformed in line with their founder's (Yvon Chouinard in the case
of Patagonia) or CEO's (Ray Anderson at Interface) personal sustainability
convictions. As a result they have both become model sustainable enterprises
and their influence has flowed far beyond the reaches of their individual
product lines and has begun to influence the bigger system. While both of
these companies also pay a lot of attention to physical details, like choice of
materials, they influence the overall system most by setting more sustainable
business goals.

1. The mindset or paradigm out of which system arises

Paradigms, or the accepted models of how ideas relate to one another, are
the sources of systems. If we influence things at the level of a paradigm, then
a system can be totally transformed. Paradigms affect ideas and thoughts and
are information led. Generally speaking, we resist changes to our paradigms
more than any other type of change, although as Meadows states: 'there's
nothing physical or expensive or even slow about paradigm change. In a
single individual it can happen in a millisecond. All it takes is a click in the
mind, a new way of seeing.'[57] Fostering this new way of seeing is the ongoing biggest challenge of sustainability for the fashion and textile sector
– to build a convincing, reflective and ethical paradigm that is more sustainable by design.

CHAPTER THREE Use Matters

Research from the Netherlands shows that the average piece of clothing stays in a Dutch person's wardrobe for 3 years 5 months, is on the body for 44 days during this time and is worn for between 2.4 and 3.1 days between washings.[1] Yet even though the typical garment is only washed and dried around 20 times in its life, most of its environmental impact comes from laundering and not from growing, processing and producing the fabric or disposing of it at the end of its life. The washing and drying of a polyester blouse, for example, uses around six times as much energy as that needed to make it in the first place.[2] Just by washing the blouse half as often, the product's overall energy consumption can be cut by almost 50 per cent, with similar savings for air pollution and production of solid waste. The message here is stark: the biggest gains in environmental performance for many fashion and textile pieces can be made by tackling the impact arising from their washing and drying. Material choices, production efficiency issues and waste also matter, but for frequently washed items they do not deliver resource savings on the same scale as influencing laundry practices. Yet while use is very important, it is a vastly under-explored area of innovation in sustainable fashion and textiles. There are very few examples of fashion and textile designers getting to grips with cleanliness, hygiene and the environmental consequences of laundering their products. What is more, there is little information about the scope and potential of designing to reduce the impact of the use phase for fashion and textiles.

This chapter addresses this imbalance and explores multiple and emerging sustainability issues associated with the use phase of fabrics and garments. It touches on washing machines and detergents, opportunities to design fabrics and garments with lower impact in use, community laundries, service design and the socially and culturally determined need to keep clean. While these themes go far beyond the traditional remit of fashion and textile design, drawing in white goods manufacturers as well as home economists and sociologists, among others, they are part of a transdisciplinary approach implicit in sustainability. After all, unless we look at a product from a lifecycle or whole-system perspective, we risk ignoring major sources of environmental impact (such as the use phase) and opportunities for innovation and change. Conversely, unless we understand issues of consumer use, whole-systems improvement is not possible. The upshot of this is an overhaul in the way designers, companies and indeed whole industries view their contribution to a product's lifecycle. In systems thinking the success of the whole entails joint responsibility for all players (weavers, finishers, retailers, detergent manufacturers, consumers, etc.) to reduce impact. This makes things like laundering habits, for example, as much a concern for designers as for those who wash clothes. It promotes a sense of shared responsibility for material upkeep and associated environmental impact reduction between those who make the fabric, those who use it and those who design and produce the machines and detergents that help us keep clothes clean.

Textiles are not all the same

At the heart of designing more sustainable fashion and textiles is a broad, flexible approach that supports a wealth of differentiated activity (as described in Chapter 1 – Material Diversity). In the case of the use phase, this flexibility is perhaps even more important because of the great differences in the way textiles and garments are used. General statements about fibres or consumers can bring only limited insight, as it is in the detail and subtleties of the human–garment relationship that areas of high impact and opportunities for big change are revealed. Thus it is important to understand the differences in lifecycle impact for different textile products and, more than that, to empathize with actual washing and drying habits and use this as the basis of design innovation.

Table 3.1 sets out a rough approximation of the distribution of environmental impact across the life of various textile products. This 'back of an envelope' guide helps assess the areas of the textile lifecycle that have most impact and where change could bring biggest benefit. For example, in the case of a cotton T-shirt, the use phase has the highest impact and the effect of reducing the energy used in washing, drying and ironing the T-shirt dwarfs the possible effects of changing production methods.[3] But for carpets, the energy and environmental impact profile is weighted very differently. Here the materials production phase is very important – approximately 71 per cent of the total energy[4] – and disposal is also high impact, meaning that innovation is best directed at phases other than use.

There are a limited, but growing, number of studies that give detailed lifecycle assessments (LCA) for textiles and clothing and these confirm the high relative impact of the use phase for frequently laundered clothing. The study most commonly referred to by companies and the literature alike is that of a polyester blouse performed in the early 1990s by consultants Franklin Associates[5] for the American Fiber Manufacturers Association (AFMA), the

Table 3.1 *A rough guide to relative impact of textile products throughout life*[6]
Key: *+ small relative impact; ++ medium relative impact; +++ large relative impact.*

	Production	Use	Disposal
Clothing	+	+++	+
Workwear	+	+++	+
Household textiles	+	+++	+
Furnishings	+++	+	++
Carpets	+++	+	++

trade association for US companies that manufacture synthetic and cellulosic fibres. The study uses an established LCA methodology and its results show unequivocally that the major part of environmental impact in the lifecycle of a blouse arises from the consumer use phase (see Figure 3.1). It concludes that as much as 82 per cent of energy use, 66 per cent of solid waste, 'over half' of the emissions to air (for carbon dioxide specifically the figure is 83 per cent) and 'large quantities' of waterborne effluents (96 per cent if measured by Biological Oxygen Demand alone) are amassed during washing and drying.

The Franklin Associates study has had a major influence on the dynamics of the sustainable textiles debate in the 15 years since its publication, chiefly by drawing attention to the role played by consumer practices in overall lifecycle performance. It is important, however, that we recognize the political currency of such studies and the ways in which business interests can influence how they are presented. LCAs have a long history of being used by companies to defend themselves against environmental requirements by demonstrating that problems are more complex than initially believed,[7] and in the early 1990s synthetic fibre manufacturers were keen to deflect rising levels of environmental scrutiny away from their business practices. The headline results of the polyester blouse LCA do just this by turning the spotlight away from manufacturers (although making polyester is far from impact free) and on to consumers, their homes and washing practices. The report's executive summary states: 'it was demonstrated that the manufacture of a particular reusable product was not the most significant consequence for an energy and environmental analysis; instead improvement measures should be aimed at the efficiency of home laundering devices. It may also be possible to develop 'easy care' fabrics requiring lower consumer maintenance. These improvements would have much greater potential benefit than improving the product manufacturing process.'[8]

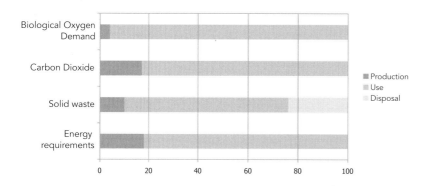

Figure 3.1 *Lifecycle impacts for a women's polyester blouse (percentage of total impact)*[9]

Spin and politics aside, LCA studies – like this one – are very important. They provide much needed, data-driven information that helps identify life-cycle stages in which environmental measures may be most effective. More than that, as practices they gain their purpose and meaningfulness from the view that environmental issues are systems extending beyond the boundaries of individual companies. In the case of the polyester blouse for example, if this information is used to galvanize action and whole-system improvement, then textile producers and white goods manufacturers, together with electricity providers and consumers, would be encouraged to work together to bring change. If this translated into 'better' laundry practices – for example, where a garment is washed on cold temperatures and dried on a line instead of in a tumble drier – then total lifecycle energy consumption could be reduced by a factor of four according to data for polyester[10] and a factor of two for cotton[11] – a substantial improvement.

Modifying laundry practices is not a guarantee of big sustainability gains across the board. If we measure the environmental impact of cotton in terms of toxicity rather than energy use, then changing garment washing and drying practices brings almost no improvement.[12] Similarly, modifying laundering behaviour brings little benefit for products that are rarely washed. This includes furnishings, carpets and some garments, typically those made from wool. Even if we wash woollen items frequently, they tend to be laundered on low temperatures and are line dried (as they are largely unsuitable for tumble drying), and so for these types of products the biggest savings can be made by improving production efficiencies, not by concentrating our efforts on use. This reiterates the complexity of the issues and also the need to think creatively and flexibly about sustainability in the fashion and textile sector. Our starting point has to be a deep understanding of user behaviour in the context of the lifecycle and to recognize which phase is highest impact. For some textile products, like furnishings, carpets and some garments, this quite plainly is *not* the use phase. For others, like cotton and polyester clothing and household textiles (cotton and polyester together account for over 80 per cent of world fibre demand), the highest impact phase is frequently attributed to use. The remainder of this chapter concentrates on the products that have a high impact in use.

Innovating to reduce the impact of the use phase

There are many ways to act to reduce the impact of the use phase of the textile lifecycle and, because the issues associated with use are systems that

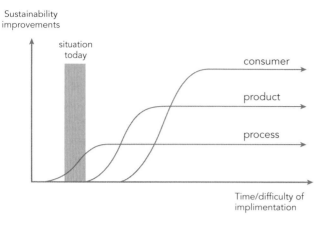

Figure 3.2 *Types of sustainable design innovation*

stretch beyond the boundaries of individual companies or industries, many of these innovations occupy brand new territory for the fashion and textile sector. They push into the world of detergents, consumer laundering habits and innovation around a product's functional and cultural meaning, and represent a massive new and emerging design and business opportunity for the fashion and textile sector. The catalyst for change will be the bringing together of knowledge and experience of parts of the supply chain that have traditionally been separate so as to ground a product in a lifecycle and work towards whole-systems change.

In this new territory of sustainable use, there are at least three broad clusters of innovations, each with a different focus. The first of these has a *process focus* and includes improved efficiency and better control of the washing process. The second treads more familiar ground to fashion and textiles and has a *product focus*, concentrating on designing fabrics and garments to cause less impact as they are laundered. The third takes a *consumer focus* and centres on designing a product's function or results and influencing the habits and values associated with cleaning our clothes. These different clusters tally with well-recognized types of sustainable design innovation[13] (see Figure 3.2) and bring a range of different degrees of environmental benefit. The more radical innovations focus on consumption patterns and bring the biggest benefits because they are based on cultural change and shifts in consumer consciousness, although they are both difficult and time consuming to influence. In contrast, changes to products or processes can be introduced more quickly as they generally involve familiar technologies and require little change to established behaviour, but they bring smaller scale improvements.

Process focus – more efficient laundering practices

Improving the efficiency of washing machines and drying techniques has obvious benefits for the use phase of fashion and textiles. White goods manufacturers and detergent companies have been aware of the sustainability impacts of their products for several decades and many have taken steps to reduce these impacts. The key issues include energy, water and detergent use in washing, and energy use in drying and ironing. Washing at a lower temperature reduces energy consumption by about 10 per cent for every 10°C reduction.[14] Eliminating tumble drying (which accounts for 60 per cent of the use phase energy) and ironing, in combination with a lower washing temperature, has been calculated to lead to around 50 per cent reduction in total energy consumption of the product.[15]

It is certainly possible to create washing machines that use water and energy more efficiently. The incentives and effect of the EU-wide mandatory energy labelling scheme for white goods bear this out and now 90 per cent of all new washing machines sold fall into the most energy efficient (A-rated) category,[16] although not all existing machines in people's homes are so efficient. Yet although manufacturers have improved the energy efficiency of appliances, increased demand driven by new products, convenience and a growing number of individual households has outstripped these gains – resulting in more loads of washing being done. Consumers' preferences for products with enhanced features, functionality and controls also limit efficiency gains. One of the UK's white goods manufacturers, for example, designed a washing machine that was able to mechanically wash clothes in cold water with comparable results to warm water washing. As well as saving energy, it removed the need for complex water heating and the sophisticated controls required to provide the range of wash programmes found in many machines, yet its simplicity meant that prospective customers saw it as backward and low status and it was never introduced to market.[17]

There are other simple solutions that help reduce the quantity of detergents used. Concentrated detergents, for example, use fewer chemicals and less packaging. Yet even though concentrated detergents are widely available, there is a move back to standard detergents (where the compact version is 'bulked up' with fillers such as sodium sulphate by up to four times volume) because of consumers' difficulties in accurate dosing and perceptions of poor value for money due to overdosing.[18] Other key issues centre on the biodegradability of detergents and whether they give rise to harmful breakdown products – which can negatively affect water quality and waterborne organisms. If stringent regulations on ultimate biodegradability were enforced it is thought that around 80 per cent of petrochemical surfactants (a key ingredient of detergents) would be banned – although one detergent industry trade body has claimed that restricting the use of surfactants because of their poor biodegradability would block the introduction of sophisticated detergents that would enable households to wash clothes with less water.[19] There are other innovations that avoid the use of detergent completely. Washing balls (reusable plastic balls placed in the drum of a machine) wash clothes by the action of the machine agitating the ceramic granules in the balls that then ionize oxygen molecules in the water. The effect, it is claimed, is to lift dirt from clothes just as a detergent would, but without any chemical additives. In a separate development, electronics giant Sanyo has developed a detergent-free washing machine that cleans laundry using ultrasonic waves and electrolysis.[20] While these machines consume significantly less energy per cycle (60Wh as compared with a standard A rating machine of 890Wh) they consume more water (110 litres per load as compared with 39 litres per load), although there is no detergent wastewater.

Dry cleaning causes a different range of environmental impacts compared to wet cleaning. Dry cleaning uses liquid solvents and detergents placed with the garment in large machines, which are then agitated to remove dirt, oil and stains. Once clean, the clothes are dried in the same machine or transferred to a separate dryer, then pressed and shaped. The used solvent is distilled so it can be purified and reused. Perchloroethylene (perc), the most commonly used dry cleaning fluid, is a petrochemical-based solvent and a hazardous air pollutant that is heavily regulated by pollution control bodies. Decades of research has shown that at high doses (higher than those used to dry clean clothes today) it affects the central nervous system and causes damage to the kidneys, liver and reproductive system after long periods of exposure. Recently a new solvent and cleaning process (Green Earth Cleaning) based on liquid silicone has been developed, although the long term health implications of this are not yet clear. Other systems are also being developed such as a detergent-free dry-cleaning system using perc, with comparable cleaning to conventional systems, that reduces environmental impacts and operational costs.[21]

The laundering process can also be made more efficient by switching away from home ownership of machines to use of community or commercial laundries. Community laundries, perhaps in the basement of a shared building, act to share washing machines between households and so reduce the number of machines in use. This cuts washing machine manufacturing and disposal costs, although it does little to address the impacts arising from the use phase of the machines. For commercial laundries, savings are not just linked to sharing machines but also to the efficiencies that come from washing continuously (including reuse of warmth and water) rather than in batches, and also from better laundry practices. Yet a number of structural barriers mean that good economic and environmental performance of commercial laundry services is difficult to guarantee. For example, the increased energy demand linked to higher washing temperatures (to maintain hygiene standards), machine drying of clothes, and transportation, mean that commercial laundry services can consume more energy than private laundering.[22] In the case of laundry services for nappies, for example, an LCA conducted by the UK's Environment Agency[23] comparing three competing nappy systems (disposable nappies; home laundered cloth nappies; and commercially laundered cloth nappies delivered to the home) concluded that, 'no system clearly had a better or worse environmental performance, although the life cycle stages that are the main source for these impacts are different for each system'.

Product focus – designing fabrics and garments that cause less impact as they are laundered

Making changes to fabrics and garments as well as to washing machines can bring improvements. Such simple ideas work to influence laundry behaviour by altering the structure and composition of garments and other textile products to promote low-impact laundering. There are a number of factors that affect how much impact the use phase of a fabric or garment causes, including washing temperature, washing frequency, size of load and method of drying. Making changes to any or all of these factors has potential to reduce impact.

In the case of wash temperature, studies reveal that different fibre types are laundered on different temperatures. Cotton items are commonly washed on warm temperatures (50°C or 60°C) whereas synthetics are washed cooler (at 30°C or 40°C). This means that by designing with 'synthetic' fibres instead of 'cotton', impact associated with the use phase of the lifecycle could be reduced, although this has complex resource implications in other areas of the lifecycle (see Chapters 1, 2 and 4) and takes little account of widely held cultural preferences for natural fibres. The more general point, however, is that selecting fibres that wash well on cool temperatures and dry quickly (without tumble drying) could bring major benefits. This gives a tentative green light to fibres like polyester and nylon on the basis of their low-impact laundering profile.

Yet the benefits of substituting one fibre for another to reduce the impact of laundering are dependent on consumers correctly differentiating between fibre types and washing them accordingly. Evidence indicates, however, that this is not the case; most people struggle to tell the difference between fibres, resulting in most textiles being laundered on cotton cycles regardless of their actual fibre content. Further complicating matters, when studies of how people *sort* their laundry are taken into account, it is clear that in the majority of cases, clothes are sorted by colour and not fibre type. These loads are then laundered at hotter temperatures if they are white or light coloured than if they are made up of dark shades. The implication here is that careful specification of colour (i.e. choosing dark shades) is an effective means of reducing the impact of consumer care. The key UK retailer Marks and Spencer has tried to circumvent laundering behaviour complexity by introducing a standard 'think climate – wash at 30°C' care label in 70 per cent of its machine washable clothes.[24] In recent years M&S has responded to increased knowledge about energy consumption in laundering by revising its clothes' recommended washing temperature from 50°C (pre-2000) to 40°C in 2001[25] and now to 30°C in 2007.

Another way to influence the environmental impact of consumer care is to reduce the volume of laundry created. Modular design can lead to less laundry, perhaps by making the parts of garments that get soiled most quickly detachable from the main body of the garment for separate washing. Of course this is not a new idea, men's dress shirts with detachable collars were commonplace in Victorian and Edwardian times until mass production led to their phasing out in the 1920s. While there are many contemporary takes on the modular design theme (such as Jun Takahashi's Paper Dolls collection for the Undercover label in 2003), none have exploited its potential for sustainability. Yet there is a major caveat that limits how effective modular design can be in reducing the amount of laundry we do – our laundry practices. Not only does modular design require consumers to get into the habit of detaching dirty parts of a garment for separate cleaning, it also has to influence the frequency with which we wash – otherwise there are few benefits. Modularity slows the frequency of washing if people wait for a full load to accumulate before doing their laundry. However, if it is done in part loads, say when dirty items are needed, then the impact is less positive – frequency is not reduced and load sizes become ever smaller.

Different options for reducing the frequency of laundering include choosing fabrics that resist soil and odour, such as with stain-blocking coatings that form a barrier around the fibre. Durable stain-resistant coatings, like

▶ Modular garments designed for low laundering

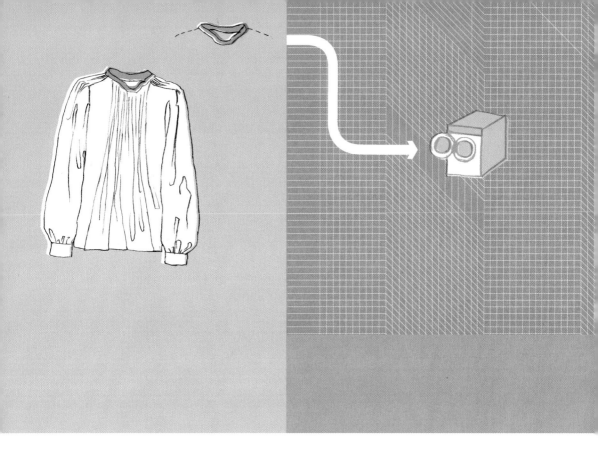

Scotchguard made by 3M, have been widely applied, particularly to dry-clean-only products like silk ties and suits, to provide resistance against oily stains and prevent the need for frequent cleaning. However, these coatings, based on perfluorinated chemicals, are known to have wide ranging human health impacts and are persistent in the environment – and face increasingly tight regulation in the future.[26]

Other coatings give antimicrobial properties to fibres. The antimicrobial agent in longest use is silver, first used in Roman times, and now gaining importance in medical textiles, making antimicrobial dressings by incorporating silver ions into highly absorbent alginate fibres. More general antimicrobial textile applications using silver depend on limiting silver's highly oxidative properties that discolour host fibres, although in recent years compounds have been developed that can be blended with fibres during extrusion to avoid this problem.[27] Antimicrobial protection can also be provided with organochlorines such as triclosan, the primary ingredient of the registered biocide Microban, suitable for polyester and nylon fibres and their blends with cotton and wool, or with coatings such as poly(hexamethylenebiguanide), suitable for cellulosic fibres. While the side effects of these bacteria killing coatings are still largely unknown, there is growing unease about the possibility that their widespread use might result in bacteria (so-called super bugs) developing resistance to drugs with the same mode of action.[28] This has resulted in the quiet removal of many of these products from retailers' shelves because of a perceived increase in product liability risks.[29] One abridged LCA study of cotton towels suggests, however, that these coatings may indeed slow down the frequency of washing by making towels stay fresher (i.e. smell fresher) for longer.[30] Yet – just as for modular clothes, above – coatings only directly influence physical factors of laundering, not cultural or behavioural ones. Statistics suggest that it is the cultural or behavioural reasons that account for most of our laundry (as only 7.5 per cent of laundry is thought to be 'heavily soiled'[31]). More dependable gains come from altering the expectations people have about how often they need to change their clothes and from influencing inefficient laundering habits, like our tendency to wash everything that is not in the wardrobe, regardless of how dirty it is.

Consumer focus – designing clean clothes

The strong interconnections between product, process and culture in the use phase makes it imperative that we work with habits, values and basic assumptions about laundering as well as with fabric composition and washing machines. This chapter concludes by exploring these issues, beginning with functional innovation.

Functional innovation is concerned with delivering results with fewer resources. The core concept is that we seek the functionality or results that a product gives us (in our case, clean clothes) and not the product itself (garment, detergent, washing machines, etc.). Recognizing this difference opens up opportunities to save resources (see Chapter 6 for a further exploration of functional innovation). Much has been made of functional innovation in the sustainable design literature and its potential to save resources (predicted at around a factor 10 (or 90 per cent) reduction in impact).[32] The benefits are thought to flow from designers working in an increased design space, no longer limited by their traditional view of what they must deliver to the customer, and because these functions frequently require cooperation across industrial sectors. A shift from thinking about products (e.g. clothes) to thinking about results (e.g. clean clothes) is a major conceptual leap for designers and businesses alike and involves a high level of interaction with users over time, far beyond the point of sale.

One way to innovate around the function of clean clothes is to design products never to be washed. While it is culturally inappropriate to keep wearing some items (like underwear) without laundering them, there are other items that are more naturally suited to 'no wash' or at the very least 'low wash' design approaches. In the No Wash top developed as part of the 5 Ways Project[33] a fine knit top was transformed into a garment designed never to be laundered. The No Wash top was designed partly to resist or repel dirt but mainly to wear it like a badge. It was developed in response to a six-month laundry diary, which documented that the key reasons for washing were smell under the arms and dirt on cuffs, elbows and front panels. The garment featured wipe-clean surfaces and extra underarm ventilation. With its bold 'decoration' of coffee spills and soap smells, it acts as a reminder of our garment's history as well as our responsibility to reduce the impact of use.

In another 'low wash' project, this time by Lauren Montgomery Devenney, a linen/silk dress was pre-stained with red wine in a semi-random splatter pattern. In this way any future stains add to the garment's design rather than cause it to be regularly laundered or even discarded. As the stains dry, their hue changes and the tonality of the stained colour gains depth.

Both of these pieces are typical of many design projects working with sustainability ideas in that they are prototypes and not in commercial production. Ann Thorpe in her book *The Designer's Atlas of Sustainability* suggests this is because these are, 'slow, engaging and connective; sometimes they're relevant only to a small local population – not suitable for "commerce as we know it"'.[34] Yet recent developments, such as a nanotechnology-based self-cleaning coating for textiles[35] – an idea reminiscent of the 1950s film *The Man in the White Suit* – have potential to mainstream low wash clothes and textiles. Ideas like designing low wash clothes fall between industries and involve forming relationships and connections where none existed before. It requires us to look in new places for inspiration, to ad hoc projects, alternative lifestyles and different people. It is very likely, for example, that we all have a durable never-washed item in our wardrobes, but probably have never recognized it as such. One starting point therefore is to identify these garment's features and design to enhance these characteristics. We also need to develop alternative ways of freshening up items in parallel with designing the garments themselves. Such tricks as hanging a garment in a steamy shower room to remove odour and 'pub smells', or learning more about how stains and smells diminish, or become more tricky to remove, over time could change practices and usher in alternative models of how to live.

▼ No Wash top produced as part of the 5 Ways Project

◀ Stain dress
by Lauren
Montgomery
Devenney

The companion solution to durable no-wash products is disposable no
wash ones (also described in Chapter 7 – Speed). Less culturally contentious
and more familiar to us, disposable textiles and clothing offer a means to
reduce to zero environmental impact arising out of washing. Just as with durable no wash items, some garment types are likely to be particularly suited
to overall lifecycle-impact reduction by designing them to be discarded
before laundering (such as underwear or items bought to be worn once only).
Yet they provide no immediate panacea, as while disposability side-steps
environmental impacts linked to laundering, other impacts, like the cost of
production and disposal, have to be included instead. To make it past the
drawing board, environmentally responsible, disposable, no wash garments
would have to be produced super-efficiently, from low-impact materials, involving a non-polluting transportation system and an effective and economic
cycle of materials reclamation and reuse. The capability of our current system
of fashion and textile production and reclamation to do this is untested, but
major improvements across the supply chain are likely if disposable no wash
products are to offer a more resource-efficient alternative across the lifecycle.

Barriers to the introduction of no wash garments are mainly organizational, technical and to a certain extent conceptual, yet the environmental
compatibility of the system is still dependent on an individual's behaviour. It
is patently obvious that the issues we are faced with in the use phase cannot
be solved simply with a technological or organizational fix. Social and cultural
aspects are at the core of deep and lasting change. And no issue is more
central to the complex relationships between people, textiles and laundering than our societal perceptions of cleanliness. Cleanliness was originally
motivated by disease prevention and even though it was quickly realized that
cleaning did little to alter the transmission and destruction of pathogens that
gave rise to many deadly diseases like tuberculosis and typhoid, it rapidly
became established as a key domestic activity. Keeping clean also became
associated with religious piety and cultural enlightenment, largely because its
opposite, dirtiness, was linked to suspect behaviour including immorality, la-
ziness and ignorance.[36] With the introduction of washing machines in the mid-
20th century, standards of cleanliness rose further. The distinction between
those who could afford washing machines and those unable to do so became
accentuated by having 'perfect' clothes. This established the link (which is still
present today) between cleanliness and social and cultural values such as success, acceptance and happiness. Keeping clean has now become an imposed
need, supported and legitimized by a multi-million pound industry and a
marketing and product world built up around an unattainable ideal of 'whiter

than white'.[37] Any changes to our laundering practices therefore impact more on ritual and symbolic needs that on material ones. This makes the dominant social status and complex cultural significance of cleanliness the key, though difficult, point to influence. Yet cultural norms change constantly and any change, however small, to cultural perceptions of cleanliness is likely to bring far-reaching sustainability benefits.

CHAPTER FOUR Reuse, Recycling and Zero Waste

In New York City, Jill Danyelle's tiny, personal fashion project Fiftyrx3[1] is to wear at least 50 per cent reused or recycled garments every day for a year. Documented daily with photographs and a blog, her style diary works and reworks her image and details her ongoing search for sustainability in fashion, art and the environment. Her principles are simple: to reuse – not bought new; to reduce – by choosing products made with environmentally friendly production practices; to recycle – making garments from a previously existing item. The results show a lavish, creative, sociable and very human exploration of cyclical living.

Different in scale and mission, outdoor sportswear producer and long time environmental pioneer Patagonia,[2] which championed the idea of making high quality recycled garments from post consumer waste well over a decade ago, is still innovating around the theme of recycling. Its polyester fleeces made from plastic drinks bottles have now become an eco-product staple. Recently it began offering shelled jackets using a recycled polyester woven fibre (reusing polyester from car dashboards and classroom chairs). More recently still Patagonia has gone one further and has started making new clothes from old through its innovative Common Threads programme. It collects unwanted polyester clothing and processes their fibres into genuine new garments using the EcoCircle fibre-to-fibre recycling system developed by Teijin of Japan. It is predicted that this fibre will save 76 per cent of the energy and 71 per cent of the carbon dioxide emissions of using virgin polyester.

Different again is LoooLo Textiles,[3] a Canadian furnishings company whose products are designed to biodegrade fully at the end of their lives. Indeed within a year of being composted the beautiful, textured blankets and cushions are reabsorbed by the earth. Ensuring complete and safe biodegradability is hard won and involves painstaking care over choice of materials and the processes by which the fabrics are made. LoooLo's products use only certified organic materials and carefully selected dyes, free of all toxic chemicals and hazardous bioproducts. The yarn used in LoooLo products is processed in a 'closed loop' facility where the spent dye baths are reclaimed and reused. LoooLo Textiles' mission is to encourage Canadian farmers towards more sustainable production as well as educating consumers about the impact their choices make.

All of these projects (and many more like them) are built around the design and business opportunities linked to textile waste. They give form to the possibilities of working with material flows and cycles and build experience of strategies like reuse and recycling. They make sustainability seem more real by infusing it with much needed luxury, availability and social acceptability, and make use of technological development, cutting-edge recovery strategies and new media (like the Internet) to assist and communicate their ideas. These projects offer an easy access point to sustainability issues and can aid a transition to a new type of society where people intuitively think in terms of loops and cascades; where waste is elevated to a thing of use and beauty; where resources can be saved; and where the hearts and minds of consumers and industry alike are prepared for bigger sustainability messages. Yet reuse and recycling also have downsides – limitations that are not connected with

▶ Windows blanket by LoooLo

the practicalities of reworking fibre, fabric and garment, but with the wasteful industrial system that they 'clean up' after.

This chapter explores the design opportunities and sustainability challenges associated with the disposal phase of the lifecycle. Waste is an important issue and acting to reduce it has an easy-won popularity that stretches far beyond the boundaries of the fashion and textile industry. The textile sector itself has a long history of working with waste. Rag collectors and shoddy manufacturers have been recovering and recycling fibre for hundreds of years. Individuals too have been reusing, repairing and reconditioning their own household textiles and garments for generations. Unsurprisingly therefore, there are a large number of designer- and producer-led initiatives focusing on textile waste and its management, mainly through reuse and recycling. These initiatives bring important benefits, particularly in the short-term, and are explored in the pages that follow. Yet longer-term waste-based initiatives hold a profoundly different challenge for the fashion and textile sector. This chapter goes on to describe a shift in emphasis from the present-day status quo that unquestioningly accepts the presence of waste as a by-product of designing, producing and consuming textiles, to a future sector where the very idea of waste itself is eradicated.

Introduction to textile waste

The total amount of clothing and textile waste arising per year in the UK is approximately 2.35 million tonnes.[4] This is equivalent to nearly 40kg per person per year, a figure that includes waste from industry and domestic sources. Only around a quarter of all waste textiles in the UK are reclaimed, with 13 per cent going to material recovery and 13 per cent to incineration. The remainder (30kg per person per year) goes to landfill, where textiles contribute to the overall environmental impact of these sites, including production of methane emissions to air and pollution of groundwater through toxic leachate.[5] Synthetic textile materials with long decay times prolong these impacts, while the decomposition of fibres such as wool give rise to especially high emissions of ammonia, a toxic pollutant to both air and water.

For the 25 per cent of UK clothing and textiles that are currently reused, the reclamation process commonly involves collecting the used products either in textile recycling banks or through a network of charity shops and door-to-door collection, then transporting them to a recycling plant for sorting. The best quality items are resold as nearly new garments in charity and second hand shops and a small proportion are reworked into customized pieces (like at TRAID Remade, see below). The majority is shipped to the used-clothing markets abroad, notably in Eastern Europe and Africa where brokers sell it to traders who then sell it on at local markets.[6] In addition to reuse of complete garments, a small proportion of textiles are recycled. They are used for wiping cloths, shredded for use as filling materials, such as in mattresses, or broken down (either mechanically or chemically) and respun into a new yarn. Approximately half of the clothing and textiles recovered are incinerated to recover energy.

In Europe, a changing legislative framework is forcing increasingly progressive recovery of textiles. Most waste textiles are considered recyclable and fall under the European Union's Landfill Directive. Recently revised targets mean that all textiles will be banned from landfill by 2015 and will have to be collected separately from other rubbish.[7] This will obviously pose considerable challenges for countries like the UK, who are faced with the task of increasing the rate of collection, and subsequent processing, of waste textiles by a factor of 3 in seven years.

Waste management strategies

The most common approach to tackling waste arising from the textile lifecycle is to implement waste management strategies (widely known as the 3Rs: reduce, reuse, recycle). Their aim is to extract the maximum benefits from products by extending their life, either as whole products, fabrics or fibres, before throwing them away. Waste management strategies intervene at the end of the industrial chain and contain or help remediate the negative environmental effects of waste generation. They work to disrupt some of the linear flow of materials through the industrial system – that is, a flow where materials are extracted from the environment at one end, are processed, used and then flow out of the system and back into the environment as emissions and waste at the other.[8]

There are different types of waste management strategies. This chapter explores three of them, organized in a hierarchy based on the relative amounts of energy and materials that are needed to carry them through. From least to most resource intensive, the strategies are:

- *reuse* of products, normally for the same purpose, sometimes with redistribution and resale;
- *repairing and reconditioning* of either whole products or parts of products to keep them useful as long as possible;
- *recycling* of raw materials to provide inputs to the manufacture of other goods.

Strategies that promote the *reuse* of goods require fewest resources, generally only involving collection and resale. *Repair and reconditioning* strategies require more resources and can involve a manufacturing infrastructure to provide parts and labour for maintenance work. *Recycling* strategies, where the products go back to fibre, or even polymer, require more resources still and are the least efficient of the strategies from a materials perspective, although in most cases they are still less resource intensive than the production of virgin materials. This hierarchy is built around maximizing embodied energy or the total energy that can be attributed to bringing that item to its existing state. Embodied energy includes the energy consumed in winning raw materials, processing them as well as transporting materials between and within these processes. The embodied energy of a garment is greater (because of its more complex form) than that of a fabric, which in turn has greater embodied energy than a fibre. The overall aim of waste management strategies is to preserve the products/materials in their highest value state (i.e. with greatest embodied energy) for as long as possible. So a hierarchy of strategies emerges: reuse of goods; repair and reconditioning of goods; recycling of raw materials.

All three strategies described above are found in the textile sector and are described in more detail below. They are all influenced by a larger trend of downcycling. This involves downgrading the quality of reclaimed materials immediately into cheap, low-value end uses rather than maintaining them as a high-value product or resource. This happens for example, when various fibres are mixed together to produce a blend of lower quality that then goes into amorphous products such as insulation panels or mattress stuffing, rather than being reused as high-value products such as clothing.

Reuse of goods

Reuse of textile products 'as is' brings significant environmental savings. In the case of clothing for example, the energy used to collect, sort and resell second-hand garments is between 10 and 20 times less than that needed to make a new item.[9] Very little of the second-hand clothing collected in the UK is reused here, most of it is shipped abroad to be sold on a global commodities market before being resold to local traders in Eastern Europe and Africa. While reuse brings resource savings, there are some concerns that the influx of cheap, second-hand clothing, particularly in Africa, has undermined indigenous textile industries. With the result that clothing collected in the West under the guise of 'charitable donations' could actually create more poverty. However, it appears that the pressure on local African producers' markets is not solely from the West's exported second-hand garments, but also from cheap imports from China.[10]

The market dominance of cheap virgin fibres and our increased consumption of them also threatens the continued economic viability of the collecting, sorting, distributing and reselling of second-hand garments and textiles in the West. Over the last 20 years, the wholesale price of second-hand textile products has been falling and at the same time there has been an enormous increase in the quantity of post-consumer textile waste produced – an inevitable by-product of growing consumption. This has led to a situation where supply of second-hand material outstrips demand and where recyclers are simultaneously overwhelmed with volume and underwhelmed with profitable markets for their product.

One small counter-trend to this is the Internet-led trade in reused goods. Here online auction houses like eBay connect users to an international source of second-hand clothes and vintage pieces, and fashion swap websites[11] allow the market in high-quality second-hand garments to flourish – although this trade is only in the top-quality branded goods that have a high resale value.

Repair and reconditioning of goods

Repair and reconditioning of textiles and garments also saves resources compared with manufacturing new items, although resource savings are less than for reuse because some labour and materials are usually needed to retrieve, fix and upgrade the products. Repair and reconditioning of textiles has been practised for generations, both in an industry context and in the home. Originally, the incentive to repair was economic; labour was cheap compared to the cost of textile materials and garments, so fabrics were carefully maintained and repaired. At home, techniques like replacing worn collars and cuffs, patching trousers and jackets, unravelling old knitwear to reuse the yarn, cutting worn bed sheets into dusters and darning holes were widely practised. Yet within two generations, the financial incentive to repair has largely disappeared, mainly because the price of new garments and textiles has fallen dramatically relative to the cost of labour. Repairing garments at home – if it takes place at all – is now motivated less by economics and more by ethical factors or lifestyle choices like down-shifting or voluntary simplicity. Repair has also been given added momentum by a revival of interest in craft skills that were once associated with the restrictive work of women, but are now reclaimed as an important creative practice in its own right by a flurry of new books about remodelling T-shirts and sweaters[12] and feminist magazines like *Bust*.

back2Back
dress by Junky
Styling

Indeed many of these same skills have become the key tools of a small but significant group of designers and producers. They use a raft of techniques such as restyling, reshaping, embellishing and over-printing to give discarded, torn and stained fabrics added value, a new life and divert (or delay) waste from landfill. For example, charitable organizations such as TRAID, under the label TRAID Remade,[13] employs a team of innovative young designers to rework and reconstruct second-hand garments by transforming them into one-off fashionable pieces that are resold. TRAID, which markets itself as a 'fashion retailer and a charity shop', has also sold its customized second-hand clothing in Top Man, the fashion retailer. And London-based outfit Junky Styling[14] has made its name by deconstructing second-hand traditional men's suits found in jumble sales and charity shops into twisted, tailored garments. Restyled and reworked clothes tend to be hand-finished and unique. They also frequently use vintage fabrics and garments, pieces that are themselves survivors, old things that have kept their value over time, and as such are easily associated with sustainability values.

Recycling of goods

As with other waste management strategies, recycling saves resources. Even the most sophisticated (and energy intensive) processes of shredding fabric, reclaiming fibres and respinning them into a yarn is thought to use less energy than the production of new items. Yet while there is a great deal of interest in recycled yarns and fabrics, there are limited products available – a fact that reflects the market dominance of cheap virgin fibres and the lack of technological innovation in the recycling industry, although this is beginning to change.

The method of extracting fibre from fabric has stayed the same for the last 200 years and involves mechanically tearing the fabric apart using carding machines. The process breaks the fibres, producing much shortened lengths, which when spun tend to produce a bulky, low-quality yarn. One way to increase the quality of this fibre is to use waste from pre-consumer sources, where quality can be more tightly controlled, or to blend it with longer, virgin fibres, as is the case with Annie Sherburne's yarn made from 50 per cent recycled London textiles and 50 per cent virgin wool.[15] Other techniques, such as that used to manufacture the yarn for Muji's reused yarn T-shirts,[16] maintain quality by avoiding mechanically pulling the fabric apart. Here cotton yarn left over on roll-ends of fabric is first unravelled and then knotted into a continuous filament ready for re-knitting. Recycled yarns and fabrics made with mechanical recycling methods remain a niche market, and it is worth noting that

◀ Reused yarn
vest by Muji

until recycled materials are regularly specified in mainstream products they will continue to be difficult to source, for without demand there is no supply. It is not enough to specify materials that can be recycled, for without a market for the recyclate, a high-value second life is unlikely.

In addition to mechanical recycling methods it is also possible to recycle synthetic fibres chemically. Chemical recycling – suitable for fibres like polyester, nylon and polypropylene – involves breaking down the fibre at the molecular level and then re-polymerizing the feedstock. While chemical recycling is more energy intensive than mechanical pulling, the resulting fibre tends to be of more predictable quality. Fibres with mixed synthetic/natural content can also be treated chemically to extract one component (normally the synthetic) out of the mixed material, so that the natural material can be reused.

The most commonly available recycled synthetic fibre is polyester made from plastic bottles. Repreve by Unifi[17] is one such example and is a 100 per cent recycled polyester yarn made from both post-consumer and post-industrial waste and can be dyed at the spun fibre stage. It has applications that range from home furnishings through to automotive upholstery and is used by Malden Mills for its recycled-content Polartec-branded polyester garments.[18] While recycled polyester gives waste from the food and drinks industry a valuable second life, there are some concerns that the material composition of plastic bottles is unsuitable for use in fabrics and garments, an example of what is sometimes called 'danger-cycling'. Plastic bottles commonly contain antimony, a known carcinogen unsuitable for prolonged contact with human skin and there have been calls for it to be replaced with readily available more benign alternatives so that in future polyester recyclate is more suitable for textile applications.[19] Recycled polyesters from other raw material sources are available, including old polyester garments produced by Teijin's EcoCircle fibre-to-fibre recycling system, although volumes are still small. Recent developments have also seen the introduction of a recycled nylon fibre, Recyclon,[20] which involves a far more challenging repolymerization process than for polyester. The fibre is made from post-industrial waste (rather than recovered post-consumer textiles), mainly substandard yarns rejected as part of manufacturing, which are then chemically reconstituted into the recycled fibre. It is claimed that producing the recycled nylon uses 80 per cent less energy than producing virgin fibre.[21]

Design for recycling and disassembly

Design for recycling (DFR) and design for disassembly (DFD) are two related approaches, developed largely in product and industrial design sectors with the explicit aim of facilitating recycling.[22] DFR and DFD initiatives have mainly resulted in the production of checklists and design recommendations that attempt to promote reuse by developing products that are easy to take apart (by avoiding glues, for example) and recycling by promoting pure (non-composite) materials that have a high resale value.

One technical factor limiting the success of textile recovery operations today is the numerous types of materials used and extensive use of fibre blends. This slows down sorting operations and forces a situation of deteriorating material quality (i.e. downcycling) that inhibits marketability of recycled material. Markets for recycled textiles are influenced by the colour, fibre type, fibre quality and the purity of the old textiles/garments themselves.[23] Thus a DFR checklist to promote optimum markets for recycled textiles would prioritize:

- white textiles, which allow easy redyeing;
- natural fibres, which are easier to 'pull' and are more versatile;
- quality (long staple) fibres, which can be processed on faster machines;
- pure (not blended) fibres that require less processing than fibre mixes and which are less problematic in subsequent processing stages.

When taken as a whole such a list represents a significant challenge to current industrial practice on a number of levels, and subverts the current design agenda by emphasizing value in resources that have finished being used over value in consumption and novelty. Yet there are trade-offs here, as while limiting the number of different textile materials in circulation may provide more lucrative markets for recycled fibres, it could promote inappropriate (and wasteful) use of fibres and encourage the increased dominance of monoculture plantations of fibre crops like cotton, with a significant environmental burden.[24] Easier disassembly of complex textile products, like garments, may be possible with developments in laser and water-jet technologies for example, where cutting, etching and bonding techniques may make it possible to 'sew' or weld fabric together without thread and so facilitate rapid disassembly at end of life.

A decade ago, vauDe,[25] the respected German outdoor gear company, developed the Ecolog system – an example of DFR principles in action. Working hard with many component and fabric suppliers vauDe put together a palette of materials that allowed their designers to develop garments that were 100 per cent polyester. This included the fabric, zips, snap fasteners, labels, thread, cords, cord grips, etc. This totally homogeneous product could then be recycled (just like a PET bottle) to make polyester resin for new products, and involves no sorting for metals or other recycling contaminates. vauDe's retailers return Ecolog products to Germany, where they are recycled with cutting-edge technology.

Critique of waste management strategies

The previous section has detailed some of the benefits that waste management strategies bring. What is more, with greater research and development, such as around techniques to extract long fibres, and certain tax breaks – say, to reduce the cost of labour for reuse and repair – these benefits could increase. Yet while waste management strategies help treat waste, containing and limiting its negative effects, they don't prevent it from being produced in the first place. This has led techniques like reuse and recycling (sometimes called eco-efficiency) to be roundly criticized as superficial and unlikely to lead to sustainability:

> Eco-efficiency is an outwardly admirable, even noble concept, but it is not a strategy for success over the long term, because it does not reach deep enough. It works within the same system that caused the problems in the first place, merely slowing it down with moral proscriptions and punitive measures. It presents little more than an illusion of change.[26]

The key charge here is that strategies like reuse and recycling fail to mitigate against fundamentally inefficient industrial systems, because they focus on optimizing one small part of the system, rather than the whole. Perversely it is almost exactly for this reason that recycling is so popular. It demands only easy-to-achieve, small change from producers and consumers alike and no radical shift in behaviour. Recycling initiatives can, for example, be bolted on to an existing product manufacturing sequence without modifying the set up. Their benefits are normally felt quickly and fit in with business and profit cycles. They require no change in what consumers buy and allow consumption to continue unabated, but just with recycled materials, not virgin ones. In some quarters this has led to a distorted view of the importance of recycling, where it is seen less as a way to manage waste (a means to an end), but more as an end or a goal in itself. The effect is for some consumers and producers to prioritize recycling over sustainability, mainly because it fits in with how things are done today. Yet recycling on its own will never bring big change. It is ultimately a *transition strategy*; useful while society is transformed into something more socially aware and less energy intensive.[27]

A different way of thinking

A new vision for reuse and recycling – glimpses of which can be seen in the projects at the beginning of this chapter – requires an overhaul of the way we think about waste and its role and value in industry. It also means a reprioritization of the value placed on end-of-pipe processes like recycling, and a profound shift away from accepting waste as an inevitable by-product of the sector to a future where we produce no waste at all. What is radical here is the shift in perspective, and not necessarily the solution. In the short term particularly, the solutions we use will probably be very familiar to us (and will inevitably rely heavily on reuse and recycling), but they will be part of an industrial system with a different goal.

An industry goal of zero waste would transform the textile industrial system at the level of a paradigm (see Chapter 2 for a discussion of change in complex systems). It would influence the whole supply chain: farmers, brokers, designers, producers, retailers and consumers. It would influence the types of materials and chemicals used, the type of product designed and how it was used. It would alleviate problems of waste mountains and overflowing landfill sites because every product would be a potentially new product and never discarded. This describes a fundamental shift from a view of the economy as a linear system where we make, produce and discard (with over 90 per cent of the resources taken out of the ground today becoming waste within only three months),[28] to a cyclical one where resources circle around the economy, becoming the source material for new goods.

Eliminating waste is a core concept of ecosystem-inspired design approaches like permaculture and industrial ecology, where everything is recycled and all waste from one component of the system becomes 'food' for another. Here what appears to be waste is actually exchange. Exchange is a liberating idea; it helps emphasize collaboration, interconnectedness, cycles and forward planning and offers opportunity for checks, balances and feedback. The next part of this chapter reviews two related design concepts based around a principle of cyclical economies and zero waste.

Industrial ecology

In its simplest form, industrial ecology aims to build societies, foster industries and develop products around ecosystem properties and dynamics, with the hope that they might be sustainable in the same way that ecosystems are.[29] This involves prioritizing materials cycles, improved material and energy efficiencies, and strategies to reduce dissipative consumption. In some instances this has led to industries being built up in clusters or dependent communities around each other so that outputs from one facility form the raw materials for another, such as in the case of the wool-scouring effluent project described below. In others it has led to a reorganization of activities to prioritize improvement of whole product lifecycles across a number of future lives. In others still, it has been used more metaphorically, where principles observable in nature, such as cooperation, interconnectedness and symbiosis, form the basis of a company's ethos.

One of the earliest examples of interconnected material cycles in fashion and textiles is a conceptual project developed in 1993 at a working conference of the international sustainable design network, o2.[30] The brief was concerned with the future provision of clothing and resulted in a multi-layered concept, where garments were made from locally produced durable materials with added 'experiential' qualities, which challenge the value and use of fabrics. Critically in the context of this chapter, the garments were also designed from the outset to be part of a cycle of use and reuse. The important idea here was to establish and plan for a hierarchy of uses for the clothes as a central part of the design: uncoloured virgin fibres in the first life produce a high quality fabric for use in high-end mens- and womenswear. In subsequent lives, fibres are transformed into bulkier and lower quality fabrics (as quality deteriorates with each recirculation) – suitable for childrenswear. In the course of reprocessing, the fibres are overdyed, transforming them into brightly coloured pieces for the children's market. While a hierarchy of use for clothes is well established on an individual level – first we wear a garment only for 'best', then for everyday use and eventually for private use at home – there is no reason that similar hierarchies could not be established across user groups. A similar idea of designing preprogrammed multiple future lives into a garment can be seen in the Nine Lives piece produced as part of the 5 Ways research project.[31] Here the garment had a preordained 'future life' ready installed and the act of transforming old into new breathed new life into a tired garment. In the first life two separate pieces were produced: a knitted woollen top and simple printed A-line skirt. In the next life they were creatively morphed into one with embroidery. Using the yarn carefully unwound from the top and the sewing guide printed as a pattern on the skirt in its first life, the user stitches into the skirt to produce a new and unique piece.

A larger scale example of a materials cycle has been established by Patagonia, mentioned in the introduction to this chapter, through its 'Common Threads Garment Recycling Programme' in collaboration with the progressive EcoCircle fibre-to-fibre recycling system developed by Teijin of Japan.

Unwanted polyester garments (including those made by its competitors) are collected from customers and transformed into fibre for use as new garments, and not immediately downcycled into lower quality end uses. This signals a departure from traditional polyester recycling routes in which high-grade polyester (such as plastic drinks bottles) is downcycled into lower value uses such as textiles, which are then further recycled into even lower grade uses, say filling materials. Instead an industrial loop offers the prospect of old garments being recycled into new garments in perpetuity. The process involves first cutting collected garments into small pieces and removing zips and buttons. Then the fabric is granulated into pellets that are chemically broken down at the molecular level and purified to produce the raw material for polyester. The raw material is then polymerized, melted and spun into new fibre in the normal way. The energy needed to fuel this process is around 25 per cent of the totals needed to produce virgin fibre, inclusive of transporting the old garments to Japan.[32]

◀ Synchilla
Snap-T fleece
by Patagonia
made with
85 per cent
recycled
content, and
completely
recyclable
through the
Common
Threads
Recycling
Programme

Data provided by Patagonia itself reveals that the environmental feasibility of Common Threads is dependent on consumers returning old garments to a service centre in as low energy a way as possible (such as by post). If, instead, a well-meaning customer drives specially to a local store to drop them off, energy and carbon dioxide savings are substantially reduced. This highlights a critical and frequently overlooked point in the design of a new generation of fabrics and garments destined for reuse, that even the most progressive technologically based solutions can be undermined by consumer behaviour. While not explicitly the case with Patagonia's Common Threads project, other trade-offs, such as the costs of collection potentially outweighing the value of the raw materials recovered, also exist. If, for example, the units are small and widely dispersed the effort worth making to recover them is less than with large items rich in resources. This means that trends towards lightweight fabrics, while saving resources in production, may end up wasting resources at the end of product life.

A very different example of industrial ecology in practice is provided by the unlikely partnership of a Yorkshire steel mill and the raw wool sludge waste from the county's wool scouring industry.[33] The Yorkshire woollen scourers produce a highly polluting effluent that has to be captured and treated, and is normally disposed of in landfill at significant cost. At the same time, and also at substantial cost, the giant steel mill Avesta Polarit was sending waste paper, cardboard and wooden pallets to landfill. The industrial ecology initiative that resulted (an industrial cluster based on waste) was brokered by a local green business network, and involved composting the scourers' wool sludge with the paper, cardboard and wood waste from AvestaPolarit in an empty warehouse at the steel mill. The resulting compost (with no apparent pesticide residues) is sold to agricultural and horticultural markets, partly as a peat-based substitute for domestic gardens. The project, which is seen as a model for cross-industrial innovation, also provides employment opportunities for young offenders and recovering drug addicts.

Cradle-to-cradle

In a linear view of a product's life, disposal is frequently perceived as the end of the line. However, the cradle-to-cradle philosophy as developed by architect William McDonough and chemist Michael Braungart[34] rejects this and extends its view of a product beyond a first life and into the next cycle of life as well – hence the term 'cradle-to-cradle'. To ensure ecological compatibility of the next life, all industrial products must be designed to fit into one of two cycles: a biological cycle – where the loop is closed by returning products harmlessly to biology/nature (through composting); and an industrial cycle – where the loop is closed by recycling non-degradable materials and products completely and continually. In effect, nature closes one loop and industry the other. Everything has to fit into one of two categories – there is no place for materials or products to exist outside of this.

The cradle-to-cradle philosophy has been applied to a growing number of fashion and textile products. The first was an upholstery fabric, Climatex Lifecycle,[35] first developed in 1993 in a collaboration between DesignTex and Swiss mill Rohner Textil. Climatex Lifecycle is designed around McDonough and Braungart's biological cycle – that is, to be completely and safely composted at the end of its life. The process of biodegradation involves the fibre being broken down into simpler substances by microorganisms, light, air or water. Synthetic fibres from a carbon-based chemical feedstock persist and accumulate in the environment because microorganisms lack the enzymes necessary to break the fibre down. In contrast, plant and animal based fibres are broken down into simpler particles, although unless chemical treatments (such as dyes and finishes) are carefully selected, they can persist in the soil after degradation, contaminating land and water with toxins released from multiple, tiny, dispersed particles. Thus the Climatex Lifecycle fabric is made from wool and ramie and is coloured with only carefully selected chemicals (out of dye manufacturer Ciba's range of 4500, only 16 were deemed suitable) manufactured without the release of carcinogens, persistent toxic chemicals,

▼ Upholstery fabric in wool and ramie by Climatex Lifecycle

heavy metals or other toxic substances. The result is a fabric that when worn can be removed from the frame of a chair and tossed onto a compost heap, where it will naturally decompose into harmless simpler substances, its next life providing 'food' for the biological system.

Other fashion and textile products have been developed around cradle-to-cradle principles and include towels and bathrobes, carpets, shirts, blouses, socks and underwear. One such product is the German producer Trigema's biodegradable T-shirt.[36] The T-shirt is made from 100 per cent cotton grown in the USA and Pakistan, chosen specifically to be free of pesticides and fertilizer residues, and the yarn is spun with natural paraffin. Trigema uses dyes that, as for Climatex Lifecycle furnishing fabric, have been specially identified to be biodegradable. A key challenge for biodegradable products is to develop all product components, including sewing thread (which is normally made from non-biodegradable polyester or polyester blends), labels, zips, fasteners and elastomeric yarn, to be compatible with the biological cycle. Research to develop biodegradable buttons, zips and spandex elastomeric yarn from corn plastics is ongoing. Another cradle-to-cradle product, this time developed as a technical nutrient textile, is Victor Innovatex's Eco Intelligent Polyester (EIP).[37] As well as being produced with 80 per cent fewer greenhouse gas emissions by lowering humidity pressures, improving heating efficiencies and implementing clean technologies throughout the operational plant, EIP is claimed to be the first antimony-free polyester that maintains its quality on recycling.

Moving forward

A zero-waste vision for the fashion and textile sector changes the goals and rules of the bigger industrial system and aligns them with sustainability. It requires a bold and innovative set of changes to the way our fibres and fabrics (as part of society at large) are designed, produced, consumed and discarded. It requires a reformulation of design priorities based around ideas of cycles where waste is reconceived as a useful, essential and valuable component of another product's future life. Changes in our approach to waste are also being encouraged by policy shifts, although these still fall short of regulating for zero waste. The EU's producer responsibility (or 'Take Back') legislation requires the original manufacturer or producer of a product to take financial and/or physical responsibility for the collection, recovery or disposal of the product after the end of its useful life, a law already on the statute book in some product sectors. The European Directive on Waste from

Electrical and Electronic Products (WEEE), adopted in May 2001, for example, requires manufacturers to ensure that 90 per cent of large household appliances and 70 per cent of all other electrical and electronic products be recovered and recycled.[38] While not in force in the textile sector yet, Take Back legislation brings a critical change of emphasis regarding responsibility for waste and gives the manufacturer incentive to create products that are more durable, recyclable and less toxic, and with reduced costs across the whole of the product lifecycle. The challenge for the sector is to transform this change in emphasis into a strong force for sustainability.

PART TWO Sustainable Fashion and Textile Systems

CHAPTER FIVE Fashion, Needs and Consumption

It's an obvious truth that the relationship between fashion and consumption conflicts with sustainability goals – although, like the elephant in the room, it's so obvious that it's often overlooked. We shop for clothes addictively and are trapped by record levels of credit card debt. The pressure to constantly re-formulate identity instigated by changing fashion trends feeds insecurity and rising levels of psychological illness. The products themselves exploit work-ers, fuel resource use, increase environmental impact and generate waste. Fashion cycles and trends contribute to very high levels of individual material consumption that are supported by the apparent insatiability of consumers' wants. We meet our desire for pleasure, new experiences, status and identity formation through buying goods – many of them clothes. And because we have an inexhaustible supply of desires, consumption – particularly of new items – continues to grow because we see the purchase of each new item as providing us with novel experiences that we have not so far encountered.[1]

This is not an inevitable destiny for fashion and textiles. They can, and must, play another role that helps us both identify the causes of sustainability problems and cultivate new aspirations. This casts fashion and textiles in a more subtle and complex sustainability role than is frequently recognized. It is a role that can never be fulfilled by a straightforward minimum-consumption drive alone. As while reducing what you buy or choosing second-hand, recycled or organic is extremely positive and tackles the impacts related to the *scale* of conspicuous fashion consumption, it does little to influence its *root causes*. This chapter builds a vision for fashion and textiles in the era of sustainability that is more than a 'can't have' anti-consumption message. Instead what follows below (and is further explored in the subsequent three chapters) is part of a 'can-do' mentality that proclaims the importance of fashion to human culture and that also recognizes the urgency of the sustainability agenda.

Value-free fashion

While fashion is at the heart of our culture and important to our relationships, our aesthetic desires and identity, the fashion and textile sector's lack of attention to moral and environmental issues is socially and ecologically undermining. Fashion, in its worst forms, feeds insecurity, peer pressure, consumerism and homogeneity, fuelled by the globalization of fashion – described as 'McFashion'[2] – where the same garment and same shopping experience is available in the New York, Tokyo and London retail outlets of a global brand. It is also implicated in serious medical conditions such as anorexia and bulimia, tragically common among young women and men, and high levels of stress linked to the need to constantly reformulate our identity each season. Not only does fashion undermine sustainability, damaging individuals and escalating consumption and disposal (consumerism is as much about individuals disposing of goods as about buying them), but fashion trends themselves have confused sustainability issues and promoted misconceptions. In the early 1990s for example, the 'eco chic' trend of 'environment friendly' garments was dominated by natural looking colours and fibres and did not reflect real-world progress. Eco chic was more a stylized reaction against simplistic perceptions of chemicals and industrial pollution than a conversion to sustainability values. Fashion collections and magazines portrayed a pure, wholesome and unprocessed visual identity for sustainability and traded on popular notions of environmental responsibility, notably that natural is 'good', and artificial, man-made or chemical is 'bad': 'With natural fibres there can be no pretence, no artifice, there is no place to hide. They are clean, simple, honest.'[3]

This message is of course simplistic and belies the complex range of environmental and social impacts associated with all textiles, both natural and manufactured. Eco chic was shape and surface detailing, image layered on top of fibre and garment. It remained separate from key sustainability concerns – and effectively promoted an illusionary visual identity for the sustainability debate of the time. Eco chic's visual message was alluringly simple and the result of an extreme case of reductionism; the sustainability message was reduced to a fibre, a colour, a texture and became so removed from its starting point that it no longer reflected sustainability ideas. The superficial beauty, language and image of fashion trivialized the real debate and skimmed over the deeper 'ugliness' endemic in the sector. This is typified by a pattern of consumption that reinforces the industry's current power structures and stymies growth of alternatives. Here disengaged, passive consumers 'follow' the trends prescribed by industry and choose between prefabricated, largely homogeneous goods. These products boost 'elitist myth production upon the catwalk altar'[4] and allow the fashion system to mystify, control and 'professionalize' the practice of designing and making clothes and further dictate how we consume them too. The result is de-skilled and dissatisfied individuals, who feel both unrepresented by the fashion system and unable to do anything about it (see Chapter 8 – User Maker).

Fashion and clothes

To bring more sustainable change we have to better understand the function of clothes. Fashion and clothing are different concepts and entities. They contribute to human well-being both functionally and emotionally. Clothing is material production; fashion is symbolic production. Although their use and looks sometimes coincide, fashion and clothes connect with us in different ways. Fashion links us to time and space and deals with our emotional needs, manifesting us as social beings, as individuals. Fashion can be what is set in motion when a designer presents a new collection on a catwalk in Milan. But equally, fashion can be the moment when a teenager crops a pair of jeans, adds a badge to an old sweatshirt and paints their Converse pumps. Clothing, in contrast, is concerned chiefly with physical or functional needs, with sheltering, shielding and protecting. Not all clothes are fashion clothes and not all fashion finds expression in garment form. Yet where the fashion sector and the clothing industry come together (in fashion clothes) our emotional needs are made manifest as garments. This overlaying of emotional needs on physical goods fuels resource consumption, generates waste and promotes short-term thinking as we turn our gaze from one silhouette, hemline and colour palette to the next in search of the next new experience. It also leaves us dissatisfied and disempowered, as physical goods, no matter how many of them we consume, can never truly satisfy our psychological needs. To change this, we need to recognize these differences and design more flexibly and intelligently. On the one hand we have to celebrate fashion as a significant and magical part of our culture (while divorcing it from rampant material consumption). And on the other we have to produce clothes that are based on values, on skill, on carefully produced fibres; clothes that are conscientious, sustainable and beautiful.

Needs

Central to this vision is an understanding of needs. As mentioned above, fashion and clothes are different entities and meet different needs. While the ostensible function of non-fashion clothing is material – to protect our modesty and keep us warm, this function changes for fashion clothes. Fashion clothes are used to signal who and what we are, to attract (or repel) others and to put us in a particular frame of mind. These emotional needs are complex, subtle and inexhaustible; where we try to meet them through our clothes, they lead to an escalation in how and what we buy. It follows therefore that understanding more about the relationship between fashion and sustainability is contingent on a greater understanding of needs. If we want to avoid depriving people of their need for identity and participation, we can't just forget about fashion and scrap everything other than the wardrobe basics. In other words, we can't radically cut consumption of clothing until we begin to understand its significance as a satisfier of human needs.

Humans possess specific, identifiable needs that are the same, regardless of nation, religion or culture. Manfred Max-Neef[5] has identified these as subsistence, protection, affection, understanding, participation, creation, recreation, identity and freedom, and they fall into two broad categories (see Table 5.1): physical (material) needs and psychological (non-material)

Table 5.1 *Fundamental human needs*

Fundamental human needs	
Material needs	Subsistence Protection
Non-material needs	Affection Understanding Participation Creation Recreation Identity Freedom

needs. Crucially, while these needs stay the same, what changes with time and between individuals is how we go about meeting or satisfying these needs. Some of us may, for example, satisfy our need for identity with fashion while others may meet this need with religion, language, work, etc. Each way of satisfying needs has different environmental and social impacts. Where these satisfiers are products or services (though they can also be social practices, forms of organization, political models and values), they are the traditional – if unconscious – focus of design.

We consume materials to put a roof over our heads, keep us warm and well fed. Increasingly we also use them to help meet our non-material or psychological and emotional needs. Here lies a paradox: psychological needs are not easily satisfied, and in some cases are even inhibited, by consuming materials alone. Thus, consuming material goods doesn't stem our desire for more material goods if we are buying them to meet psychological needs. Many of us will, for example, be familiar with the feeling of a new want or desire surfacing no sooner than the first one is satisfied. Put simply, consuming materials gives us a false sense of satisfying our psychological needs – a fact long recognized by many religious communities, as seen in their guidelines for living materially simple but active and spiritually rich lives. This point is further reinforced by a number of studies that suggest we are no happier now than in the 1950s, even though we own far more material possessions. Max-Neef stresses that needs are met by a combination of internal and external means, yet in our society most satisfiers come from sources outside of ourselves (like products), with very little attention placed on internal means such as personal growth.[6] The pursuit of commercial opportunity has drawn psychological needs into the market place and replaced internal means of meeting needs with products. Marketing techniques have been perfected that link products (like fashion clothes) to non-material needs, and where the consumption of fashion is a way to signal wealth, identity and social status and experience new things.

Understanding needs helps us understand why fashion is important to us. According to Max-Neef, any fundamental need that is not adequately satisfied reveals a poverty. Just as people are poor when they have insufficient food and shelter to meet their need for subsistence, poverties can also be experienced in relation to other needs. We are poor if we experience bad healthcare, domestic violence, etc. (a poverty of protection); and poor if we can't for reasons of widely dispersed family groups, oppression, etc. meet our need for affection. We are also poor if we cannot satisfy our need for identity, participation and creation – three needs which can (at least in part) be met by fashion. Yet fashion clothes as we experience them today are also the cause of multiple poverties: impairing the possibility of garment workers to meet needs of subsistence, protection and freedom due to low wages, forced overtime, sexual harassment, etc.; damaging our collective rights to enjoy a safe and convivial natural environment through toxic pesticide use and chemical pollution; and inhibiting our need to participate, understand and be creative by being sold 'closed' ready-made products with little opportunity for self-expression.

Our challenge instead is to build a new vision for fashion that satisfies needs and minimizes poverties. To do this we must first understand what represses or stimulates opportunities for meeting needs. Then we must apply this understanding so that we minimize negative effects and maximize positive ones. To minimize the negative effects, we can begin by making simple changes such as switching to Fair Trade and organically grown materials. To maximize positive ones we can establish decentralized local production facilities and promote participative design between user and maker. This changes the emphasis of our practice away from producing goods that undermine us and the health of our environment and society and onto those that nurture our well-being. Max-Neef describes this as a shift from a system where 'life is placed at the service of artefacts (artefacts are the focus) … to [one where] artefacts [are] at the service of life (quality of life).'[7] This simple shift changes the goal of the industrial system. It is a distinction between a culture defined by its material consumption and one that is catalysed by using material and non-material satisfiers to help us engage with, connect with and better understand ourselves, each other and our world. John Ehrenfeld has described this as *flourishing*:

> …our artefacts need to be designed to support conscious choice and reflective competence rather than blind consumption. They should produce long-lasting human satisfaction… We will be able to flourish simply by living life as we encounter it.[8]

▶ *Caress Dress produced as part of the 5 Ways Project*

Designing and making fashion clothes that help us 'flourish' would transform the textile industrial system at root. Not only would it change what we design and produce, it would also influence consumption. Max-Neef suggests that if we promote a broad understanding of needs that recognizes the importance of internal as well as external means of meeting them, then we can start a process of transformation that draws us out of a narrow focus on material wealth (what we do or don't have) and instead motivates and mobilizes people to use their own skills and ideas to satisfy their needs (see Chapter 8 – User Maker).

Designing fashion to help us flourish is extremely challenging. A wide range of examples of this new type of fashion can be found in the chapters that follow. One project that specifically worked with Max-Neef's ideas of needs was Super Satisfiers,[9] part of 5 Ways Project. Super Satisfier's aim was to develop a concept piece that explored the way we meet needs by converting subtle and unconscious uses of clothing into a design brief. The hope was that this would imbue a garment with more meaning to try to break the cycle of consumption and dissatisfaction and make our hidden needs more obvious so that we can connect more with ourselves. The project focused on the need for affection and developed the 'caress dress' – one designer's highly personal take on how she attracts attention from others through garments. The dress uses slits and subtle cut-aways to reveal hints of bare skin at the shoulder, the waist and the small of the back. Its purpose is to invite friends to touch and embrace her and for the wearer to feel the warmth of others' affection for her.

Needs and satisfiers are both complex and extremely personal. Each of our psychological needs is met in different ways and what is nurturing for one of us is frustrating for another. So if we pursue a needs-based approach to promoting sustainability, then we have to build an industry that respects – and actually finds business opportunity in meeting – our diverse, individual needs. To do this effectively, we need to recognize that products only play a partial role in meeting needs and that the majority of human well-being lies entirely outside the product world. This does not mean that products and the industrial sectors that produce them aren't part of a needs-based approach; only that they aren't all of it. There is also a key role in needs-centred design for the public sector and community groups in fostering different types of social practices and forms of organization.

A new fashion ethic

What will fashion that helps us flourish be like? As hinted at above, it will have to be responsive to our diverse, individual needs. Diverse products do far more than just showcase lots of different materials (see Chapter 1); they can also sustain a sense of ourselves as human beings by being more likely to recognize a wide range of symbolic and material needs. Smaller makers with flexible production systems can produce products that are personal and specific and that are just right for us. They reject homogenization and autonomy in favour of expressiveness and difference. This necessitates a different production system, one where industry is made up of 'millions of markets of dozens' (a plethora of small volume products), rather than our present-day set-up of 'dozens of markets of millions' (a limited number of large volume products). This more needs-friendly approach to production happens also to chime with predictions for the future of business more generally, which make use of new media and tools like the Internet to match consumer needs with specific products. This is the complete opposite of the Fordist way of doing business so dominant in the 20th century, where a few generic products were marketed to all people.

The success of this diverse, flourishing fashion ethic will also be secured in the relationships it fosters. We will see beauty and greatness in garments that value process, participation and social integration, in pieces that advance relationships between people and the environment. The activity of friends knitting together is beautiful, compostable garments are beautiful, supporting a disadvantaged community with careful purchasing is beautiful. Relationships can be fostered by designing garments that encourage us to ask deep questions about our sense of place in the natural world. Such garments could accomplish this by supporting our desire to ride a bike instead of taking the car, or by being shareable between friends. Sustainable fashion is about a strong and nurturing relationship between consumer and producer. It is about producing garments that start a debate, invoke a deep sense of meaning or require the user to 'finish' them with skill, imagination or flair. It is about designing confidence- and capability-inducing pieces that encourage versatility, inventiveness, personalization and individual participation (see Chapter 8 – User Maker).

This unorthodox agenda is a call to get 'back to roots' and in essence describes a future for sustainable fashion that *reconnects us with nature* and *with each other*. It works at many different levels: individual and industry, emotional and material, fashion and fibre. Sustainable fashion must encourage our sense of ourselves as human beings and revitalize our relationships with others, including those who make our clothes, and so will work to counter our lack of awareness of poor working conditions, poverty wages and poor environmental standards. It will emancipate us from a submissive dependence on fashion by instead giving us the skills to creatively participate with and rework our clothes. We have to become activists, skilful producers and consumers of garments, our actions exploding some of the mystique, exclusivity and power structures of the fashion system to break the link between fashion and material consumption and to offer alternative visions of fashion's future.

A new aesthetic

A vision of fashion that is based on needs and relationships is inevitably different to today's way of doing things. Today many of the products we see on the rails on the high street, or catwalk shows of the elite brands, reinforce the idea that it is possible – and even desirable – to be ethically and politically neutral and separate from the world, and to aspire to design values of objectification and egocentricity. Yet it is impossible for us to detach ourselves from the political aspects of our work. We are part of the natural world, not separate from it, and have a shared path with reciprocal actions: while we impact hard on nature, nature also influences us. Giving form to this connectedness and reciprocity is a key part of sustainable fashion. Aesthetics are important to sustainability because they act as a great social attractor, an outlet for ideas, a form of cross-referencing and an agent of change. Ezio Manzini suggests that aesthetics give direction to the choices of a great number of individuals.[10] It follows from this that by making the sustainable alternative more attractive to people, we can encourage them to willingly embrace it.

The way something looks is also linked to understanding and knowing and is therefore critical to sustainability. As the opening line of John Berger's classic text *Ways of Seeing*[11] states: 'Seeing comes before words. The child looks and recognises before it can speak.' Thus in 'seeing' sustainability in, say, a permaculture garden, a community market or an engaging, responsible garment we begin the process of understanding it. This process happens on an emotional and intuitive level – even before sustainability is explained we have some insight. It follows from this that we must use and value this potential, as this 'experiential' knowing is key to a richer, deeper and more true to life understanding of sustainability. Knowing about things because of an experience is recognized as one of the 'four ways of knowing' used to explain how we know something beyond the traditional reaches of scientific and academic study. The four ways of knowing are experiential, presentational, propositional and practical, and are said to have most value when they build on each other, that is, when 'our knowing is grounded in our experience, expressed through our stories and images, understood through theories which make sense to us, and expressed in worthwhile action in our lives'.[12] This transformation of an intuitive and empathic understanding of the world through to informed making maps nicely onto the ways many designers work.

As it stands today it is difficult to see or sense sustainability in many of the fashion and textile products available. But perhaps we simply do not know what we are looking for. Eco chic graphically reminds us that the sustainable aesthetic is not based on arbitrary notions of styling, superficial differences and indiscriminate detailing; after all, most fibres can be processed to look 'pure', 'natural' or 'recycled', regardless of their true provenance. Indeed, perhaps as a reflection of the fact that fibres can look identical regardless of whether they are conventionally or fairly traded, coloured with traditional or low salt dyes (etc.), most sustainable fashion pieces are aesthetically indistinguishable from everything else on the market – in fact, this is some designers' express intention. This has both good and bad implications. The implications are good if the product is allowed to trade on its own merits, rather than as an 'issue' product, where its success is linked to the popularity of the 'issue' at stake; and good if it means that a product is not tainted with some of the negative preconceptions of green design, such as poor quality and high price. The implications are bad, however, if the appearance of a sustainable fabric or garment is purposely limited to comply with today's aesthetic models, just to make it 'fit in'. These models after all are based on production systems that are widely regarded as value-free and where the subtext of social and moral responsibility is missing.[13] Today's production systems do little to support a sense of relationship either between people or nature, they care little about how or by whom and in what conditions products are made, or the speed with which they are consumed. Long-term sustainability requires a switch to an aesthetic that instead of being value-free becomes based on values and takes its form from these values, not from how things look today.

For the artist and author Suzy Gablik,[14] the form that sustainable products take is rooted in an individual or a particular place, and yet it is not static, but constantly evolving into a new relationship with society and nature. This emphasis on strong roots and active partnerships means that key sustainability values include: *community*, where a new relationship is fostered between designer, producer and consumer; *empathy*, that is the capacity to share what another is feeling and to recognize this understanding as being part of a connection to the bigger system; *participation*, where we devolve fashion's power structures and take a more active role in its production; and *resourcefulness*, where we find opportunity in reducing the consumption of materials, energy and toxic chemicals.

Perhaps one of the best examples of this new aesthetic is found in the West Wales' clothing company, Howies[15] – both in its business model and the products themselves. Howies was established in 1995 by Clare and David Hieatt, who started their business in a spare room, making T-shirts for BMX riders.

SPORT SETS
YOU FREE

Since then the company has grown to employ around 20 people and is now 'Cardigan Bay's third biggest clothing company'. Its emphasis on its small size, its strong links to its community of sports, and its Welsh roots permeate the company's values. Howies' aim is to make people think about the world they live in. Its products, designed for functionality, simplicity and durability communicate this culture of questioning and respect for the environment through carefully selected materials, slogan T-shirts, and a web presence and mail order catalogue that are as much about social comment and compassionate responsiveness as about selling clothes. Its aesthetic is pragmatic, goal directed and charged with ethical sensitivity.

▲ Organic cotton T-shirt and jeans by Howies

Reversing the escalators of consumption

The process of transforming our industry into something more sustainable – and more sensitive to our needs – takes time. It is a long-term commitment to a new way of producing and consuming that requires widespread personal, social and institutional change. In the shorter term, there exist other, more easily won, opportunities to tackle consumption patterns, such as those that come from subverting well-recognized social and psychological mechanisms that induce blind, buy-as-much-as-we-can consumption. This can help buy us time while we build a greater understanding of the way goods meet our needs, and constrain, distort or enhance the quality of our lives. This chapter concludes with a review of some of these consumption escalators, namely:[16]

- the pressure to compare ourselves to others, such as through the accumulation and display of possessions;
- the rolling replacement of things, as each new purchase requires the buying of another to 'match';
- the cultural obligation to experience everything and buy things accordingly;
- constant consumption as part of a continuous process of identity formation.

Perhaps one of the easiest places to start the process of slowing consumption is to piggyback on already existing trends and steer them in the direction of sustainability. Trends such as those for informalization or eclecticism, for example, have potential to influence the pace of consumption. In the move towards more informal ways of living, the relaxing of rules and codes of dress in both social and business contexts leads to less specialization and more crossover between use of products. Amplifying this, designers can develop

▼ Green contrasting stitching on organic cotton T-shirt by American Apparel

products that suggest a wealth of different use opportunities (multiple functions or shared products) to help reduce the quantity of what we buy.

The trend for eclecticism encourages people away from feeling impelled to sustain 'coherence' across all fields of behaviour and have a matching family of products for all occasions. Resources can be saved by instead mixing and matching a range of pieces including second-hand, organic, craft (etc.) in addition to conventional garments. Here the potential to reduce impact comes from using more sustainable pieces alongside already existing ones.

It also comes from designers working in new roles, including as 'cultivators' of widespread social innovation – developing the confidence of consumers to ask questions, buy from a range of retail forms (for example, from second-hand shops, the Internet and high street brands) and to work and rework their existing wardrobe.

Other consumption escalators have the potential to be slowed by introducing lower impact products. Where the pressure to consume is driven by *identity formation*, we regularly redesign ourselves by purchasing new items or forming new associations. If these associations are with sustainability, then we may feel compelled to buy ethical or organic across the board. This is an escalator catered for by ethical supermarkets that offer a complete range of alternatives.

If the pressure to consume is driven by *display* of 'green' goods, then it is likely that these have to be highly visible, like for example, solar panels emblazoned on the roof of a house, rather than loft insulation hidden from view. In this case, each 'green' product also has to be designed with an identifiable and visible mark to communicate this difference. This could be achieved with logos and labelling, such as the energy labels included on washing machines; buttons, as used by the Made-By supply chain traceability initiative (see Chapter 2);[17] or with stitching – American Apparel for instance sew their organic cotton line with distinctive green contrast stitching. Importantly, the pressure to consume driven by identity formation does not necessarily require the consumption of materials, but rather access to a throughput of new products. One potentially more resource-efficient way to lessen the impact of this drive to consume is to shift to a service economy, where materials and goods are used not owned (see Chapter 6 – Local and Light).

Service design could also help counter the negative consumption effects of buying things to experience *novelty* and *variety*. Here products would be leased for short periods, returned when their novelty wears off, and replaced with a new hire good. Designing products for lease in this way is relatively unexplored in the fashion and textile sector, outside formal dress hire or hospital and hotel linen services, and offers major sustainability potential. Modular products also have the potential to suppress the consumption mechanism for novelty and variety. Here we would ensure newness and variation by developing products with a flexible core, adaptable sections and removable portions that grow and change over time. Modularity has been explored by many designers, including Rei Kawakubo at Comme des Garçons, and Jun Takahashi in the 2003 paper dolls collection for the Undercover label – where aprons of clothing were fixed with Velcro tabs on basics. The use of new technologies such as wearable electronics also has potential to reverse consumption for

▶ Modular concept top formed by construction of hexagonal fabric pieces that can be removed and replaced when needed or completely deconstructed and rebuilt by Ariel Bishop

the sake of novelty, though with as yet unknown environmental side effects. For example, garments are in development with an electronic interface that would allow new images and colours and even different garment shapes to be downloaded onto a piece – resulting in many new and different garments in one.[18]

In the last part of this chapter, we have seen a little about how we can use consumption escalators to influence what and how we buy. As designers, if we can build on this and also begin to understand how the way we go about meeting our needs and the goods that are available to us constrain, distort or enhance the quality of our lives, then we can begin to think of ways to develop sustainable fashion that nurtures us and our relationships. Then we will begin to give form to a culture where quantity is superseded by quality. The following three chapters further explore this new culture of sustainability.

CHAPTER SIX Local and Light

Many of the issues at the heart of the fashion and textile sector's unsustain-ability are linked to the scale of production and consumption and its use of resources. Large-scale production, global trade and internationally available goods impact hard on resource flows and producer communities, and deliver goods to consumers that rarely reflect local materials, skills and fashion preferences. Meanwhile high volume production and consumption mean that we buy and discard more than ever. This chapter explores sustainability opportunities linked to a new view of scale and resource use in fashion and textiles: designing local and designing light. Designing local is concerned with developing a sector with a greater sensitivity to place and scale; a sector devised to sustain communities and support jobs while protecting the quality of the environment. Designing light is focused on promoting resourcefulness in production and consumption. This gives rise not only to lightweight materials and structures but also to lighter, less material-intensive ways of organizing consumption, like shared products and services.

Local and light are both principles derived from ecosystem properties and dynamics. Natural forces and processes tend to evolve and self-organize to maximize lightness and minimize materials and energy use, 'curbing excess from within'; most biological systems use local expertise to produce the materials it needs and process its waste. This chapter begins its exploration of the potential of local and lightweight design as a creative force for change in fashion and textiles with a short introduction to their common starting point, nature-inspired design and specifically biomimicry.

Biomimicry

While imitating or copying nature is not a new idea, the science and potential of biomimetic design has developed rapidly over the last decade. In her seminal book *Biomimicry*,[1] Janine Benyus talks about biomimicry's three approaches: the first using nature as a model to inspire approaches that solve human problems; the second using nature as a judge or measure of the 'rightness' of our innovations; and the third, nature as mentor, looking metaphorically at us designing with values and perspectives present in the natural world. Biomimicry has a long history of influencing textile products – indeed perhaps the most commercial biomimetic product of all is Velcro, first patented in the 1950s by Swiss inventor George de Mestral after he noticed how burrs stuck to his woollen trousers and his dog's fur while out walking. He discovered that each burr consisted of hundreds of tiny hooks that 'grabbed' into loops of thread or fur, and subsequently set about developing a hook and loop tape as a strong, reusable fastening system. More recently the same approach of copying features of plant or animal design was used by swimwear manufacturer Speedo,[2] who developed a fabric and full body swimsuit, Fastskin FSII, which was inspired by the way a shark's skin reduces friction and channels the water over the body as it moves through the water.

Other biomimetic products, like the pigment-free coloured fibre Morphotex,[3] bring specific sustainability benefits. Developed by Teijin, Japan, and inspired by the iridescent morpho butterfly of South America, Morphotex achieves its colour by causing light to diffract and interfere with the fibre in ways that amplify certain wavelengths. This creates brilliant colours to the viewer through the use of physical structure rather than with pigment or dye. In effect, the surface layers play with light and produce a coloured fabric without the energy and resource impacts associated with dyeing and printing. The Morphotex fibre has a multilayer stack structure made up of 61 layers of polyester and nylon, each with different refractive indexes. By controlling the thickness of the layers it shows variations of the four primary colours, red, green, blue and yellow, dependent on the angle and intensity of light.

Yet perhaps the greatest contribution of biomimicry ideas to sustainable fashion and textiles is that it provides a new set of ideas and language for how to interact with, innovate and develop fibres and fabrics that are as sustainable as the natural systems they are modelled on. In *Biomimicry*, Benyus introduces a way to judge whether our innovations are 'good' for us. She states that a good innovation will answer 'yes' to the following questions:[4]

- Will it fit in?
- Will it last?
- Is there a precedent for this in nature?
- Does it run on sunlight?
- Does it use only the energy it needs?
- Does it fit form to function?
- Does it recycle everything?
- Does it reward cooperation?
- Does it bank on diversity?
- Does it utilize local expertise?
- Does it curb excess from within?
- Does it tap the power of limits?
- Is it beautiful?

Many of these themes are touched in this book. This chapter now explores opportunities for 'good', bio-inspired innovation specifically in two of these areas: local and light.

Local

The global market in textile production means that many textile products are transported several times between processors before a product reaches a user – indeed it is thought that the average T-shirt travels the equivalent distance of once around the globe during its production.[5] In transportation, a fabric uses local resources and causes local pollution, both of which are seen as costs 'external' to the product, and are not passed on to the consumer. One American study[6] priced these transport-related costs for a cotton T-shirt, moved between different growing and processing regions of the USA. It concluded that the environmental cost of transportation was significant and amounted to about half the cost of growing the cotton and 16 times its processing cost – a figure likely only to increase as more fabrics and garments are processed offshore and in the light of predictions about the continued growth of China's manufacturing capabilities; it is thought that by 2008 China will be responsible for more than half of the world's textile and garment production.[7]

But reducing carbon emissions from transportation is only one part of the move towards local; the others are concerned with economic resilience, social engagement and cultural and aesthetic diversity. If we look to parallels in the natural world we see that most biological systems operate locally, or as Benyus puts it, 'nature doesn't commute to work'.[8] Nature – with the exception of migrant species – 'shops' locally, using local expertise to produce the resources it needs and process its waste. Many sustainability initiatives have sprung up from local actions and the grass roots; indeed, few ideas are more ecologically powerful than those linked to designing and developing products to sustain communities – providing people with meaningful work and a sense of connection with the place and the people with whom they live.

Localism is an antidote to unsustainability. According to David Pepper, 'revising the scale of living will solve at root many of society's theoretical and practical problems'.[9] Why? Because in small communities people see and sense the effects of their own actions on each other and the environment and are quicker to enjoy the benefits of change. Pepper also suggests that the division of power based on area is predicted to best promote, 'equality, efficiency, welfare and security in all society. This will produce more cohesion, less crime, more citizen participation in government and sensitivity to the needs of others.'[10] Local action also helps develop human creativeness as we inventively respond to problems with the resources and expertise that is to hand. The result is a less homogeneous or cloned society, one which reflects the ideas, skills and resource flows of a local place and an aesthetic agenda – be it of buildings, food or clothes – that grows from the ground up and is not set by and for the convenience of big business (see Chapter 1 – Material Diversity). Local products inspire and challenge the community while at the same time creating jobs and making use of local resources. Other designers acknowledge the importance of the local agenda. McDonough and Braungart, for example, talk about the 'best' product being one with a human and material engagement with place.[11] For John Thackara, the 'best' product is one that makes citizens look at their community with fresh eyes.[12] For Stuart Walker, the 'best' product creates work at the local level that is socially enriching and economically viable in the product's production, use and disposal.[13]

Locally made, globally relevant

Localism represents an opportunity for major change; an opportunity to design for distinctiveness, limited editions, and fibre grown within, say, 50 miles. It presents us with an occasion to produce and consume based on more sustainable models that recognize natural limits and the importance of reliable work to strong and resilient communities, while affirming the central role fashion and textiles plays in our culture. Yet localism poses very particular challenges for fashion and textiles. In a globalized world, no industry is more broadly dispersed around the planet than textiles and apparel. Just as the textile industry led the industrial revolution, fashion and textiles has been among the first sectors to be part of today's international division of labour. As such, truly local products are rare and getting rarer – as are the small-scale, regional, specialist spinners, weavers, knitters, dyehouses and tailors who once dominated global production. Yet no one is suggesting that local production will replace global production, but rather that it will complement, learn from and then, in time, begin to influence it. Some global production pressures, such as the push to cut lead times, increase speed-to-market of a design and rapidly respond to consumer trends, are actually cutting the distances textiles and garments are transported. Zara, for example, produces its clothes in Spain and Portugal, near to the markets of Europe, and while this adds a price premium to their clothes due to higher labour rates, it avoids expensive stock build-up and waste. Yet while this saves on fuel, consumer choice is still limited. For robust social and environmental standards we need to move away from a monoculture of globalized production dominated by the power, concentration and international reach of big business. Local helps us do this by infusing our production with the idea of scale. A properly scaled production system allows a diversity of alternatives to thrive and means that wealth is not concentrated in the hands of the few.

Contrary to what some may think, local and small-scale is not simplistic or sentimental – in fact making things locally is frequently more complex than its one-size-fits-all alternative. Neither is local corny or rustic – just because local products are designed and made at decentralized factories far away from fashion capitals, using regional-specific materials or traditional tech-

niques, does not mean that they are not a part of the global fashion system. Their diversity and complexity comes from networking multiple small makers and their success lies in cultivating the strengths of local production (diversity, closeness to audience, traditions) while carefully connecting it to the information flows (fashion symbols and iconography) of the global network (the fashion system). One of the best examples of local production with global fashion system cachet is Alabama Chanin[14] and its previous incarnation Project Alabama, for which Natalie Chanin initiated a series of US-based community revitalization projects that combine old-world craft with couture style and reuse of materials. She employs local women – former factory workers, retired teachers, widows, housewives and secretaries – to help sew one-of-a-kind, handmade garments for her fashion line. Gathering together to work in circles reminiscent of Alabama's dwindling tradition of quilting, the women forge friendships while stitching, embroidering and beading Chanin's much coveted designs. Chanin initially used only vintage fabrics found at local charity shops, then relying on bulk shipments from the Salvation Army to fill all the orders. She prepares her seamstresses for the task with lessons of mindfulness, instructing them to handle the thread with love as they sew. She believes that, 'If you love your thread, it brings something to the wearer.'

▲ Skull dress by Project Alabama

Local and connected

The Internet and other new technologies have helped revolutionize the network potential of local by driving down the costs of production and distribution. One effect is to better connect consumers to the right product for their specific needs while allowing small independent producers to make money from their highly specialized items. Other changes include the evolution of 'open source' projects like Wikipedia and YouTube, where groups of people form active cooperative networks, organizing themselves to solve problems and practise the solutions they want (open-source initiatives are explored further in Chapter 8). *Sustainable Everyday,*[15] Ezio Manzini and François Jégou's exhibition and book of the same name, builds on the theme of local and connected, drawing together a whole series of 'living strategies' that offer sustainable alternatives for urban living from ten different countries. The result is a collection of cosmopolitan ideas of local origin, focused on small, local systems change, that when connected together bring the potential of big systems transformation.

Other types of technological developments are also revolutionizing the potential of the textile sector – and crucially also the mass market – to respond more locally. The digitization of production – for example, where computer-aided design (CAD) technology is interfaced with whole-garment knitting machines, body scanning technologies and digital printing – makes possible the 'mass customization' of garment production at multiple locations, perhaps even in stores and in collaboration with consumers.[16] Mass customization is concerned with best fit rather than exact fit and tries to find the closest match for a consumer's needs from a selection of predefined options rather than making individually tailored garments. One of the best examples of mass customization is provided by Adidas's sports footwear service (miAdidas)[17] that uses modular components to provide a 'best fit' for the consumer. A miAdidas shoe is made from pre-manufactured parts selected for best fit via foot scanning. The service uses a web interface and virtual viewer, and when happy with the fit the user can choose up to 100 variations of design. At present the mass-customized shoe costs 50 per cent more than a standard shoe. To date 100,000 shoes have been made, with a less than 1 per cent reject level.[18] In another example, Lands' End,[19] the USA's largest catalogue sales company, has also explored mass customization for its products. Trials with body scanning proved uneconomic (as the process is slow – around 15 minutes – and labour intensive) but, through its 'custom' service, information about a customer's size is used to adapt standard patterns and produce garments cut and sewn in single units using modular manufacturing techniques.

Some technologies, however, are not viable at the local level – instead local production will prioritize different processes and perhaps combine premanufactured pieces together with local expertise, to begin to use the flexibility and skill of regionally distributed human creativity with some of the resource efficiencies brought by producing large volumes centrally.

Local wisdom

The knowledge and experience of those who discover things by living and working in one place can bring a wealth of new perspectives and practical solutions to many environmental and social problems. Local wisdom rarely influences business agendas yet it has the potential to generate solutions that solve the problems of millions of people. In India, Professor Anil Gupta, of the Indian Institute of Management and founder of the Honey Bee Network,[20] collects village wisdom by walking between rural communities, gathering local lore, knowledge and innovations on the way and so far has posted 50,000 of these village sustainability ideas on the Internet. These walks, or journeys of discovery (Shodh Yatra), involve Gupta and his entourage 'seeking solace at the feet of creative people' – recognizing, honouring and giving credit to the creative grass roots, which in India's case is the rural poor. The local wisdom that emerges typically uses few materials but an abundance of experience and ingenuity. It also has other basic characteristics, such as ease of making and repair, energy efficiency and production of little waste. Gupta sees the very act of gathering these local ideas as a transformative act, building confidence while both recognizing and encouraging a community's potential. Local wisdom involves looking to the margins for the alternative views of creativity necessary for sustainability.

Distinctiveness

The local agenda is concerned with products that enhance diversity, celebrate traditions, build communities, create meaningful employment and respect local environmental conditions – it is a combination of product, skill and emotional investment. At the local level it is possible to work closely with users and to develop new or reinstitute old styles as appropriate, to adjust designs or processing techniques to fit new needs and build a job-rich infrastructure for repair and reuse. The essence of localism is distinctiveness and our task is to not only preserve this but also make it grow. But what exactly is distinctiveness? Building on its substantial experience gained from working at the local level, the New Economics Foundation has drawn up some guidelines for distinctiveness,[21] which offer countless opportunities for design innovation:

- Distinctiveness is not neat, it is fuzzy, overlapping and necessarily inclusive.
- Local people have primacy: if they feel a place is distinctive, then it is – and this can be used to draw in outsiders.
- Distinctiveness must be authentic: what is distinctive is not usually susceptible to marketing unless it has genuine roots – often historic roots – in the places where it is claimed.
- Assets are more than just economic: they might be a communal memory about a place or a sense of good neighbourliness. They will not always be assets that can be exploited economically, though they may make economic exploitation easier.
- Small things are as important as big things: it is the texture that makes a place authentic as much as recordable economic assets, and very small changes can enhance people's sense of distinctiveness as much as anything that requires major investment.
- Distinctiveness requires a sense of responsibility: building distinctiveness normally requires new local institutions or practical

alliances capable of bringing local stakeholders together to make
things happen.

- History gives depth to a place: it gives added dimensions – but it has
  to be about history alive and well today, rather than just about the
  past, which leads to deadness.

Local examples

Localism requires us to begin to adapt our appetites to where we live; and to
celebrate this as a necessary companion to globalized production. Shopping
locally requires a local knowledge that few of us have any more. Who among
us knows what we would wear if we had to grow and process fibre and fabric
locally? And why are examples of products with discrete local identities so
rare? The answers are beginning to be formulated by an emergent and ever
more visible group of entrepreneurs, who are building products and businesses that suit the land and the local culture and utilize the skill-sets of people
who live there. Some of these groups have begun to use the concept of
'clothes miles',[22] trading on the now familiar idea of 'food miles' – a method
of communicating 'hidden' transport-related emissions and fossil-fuel consumption in the food industry – to promote a sense of an alternative to global
production. Knowing more about our history, community and our 'natural address' gives us important starting points from which to develop different ways
of clothing ourselves.

BioRegional,[23] an independent environmental organization that is focused on developing sustainable products and services, has invested years of
research into growing traditional fibre crops in the UK for use as local textiles.
The climatic conditions of BioRegional's natural address – the south-east of
England – favour the growing of hemp – a crop that in the 16th century was
grown by every farmer in the UK, by order of an act of parliament introduced
by Henry VIII to ensure the supply of sails and ropes for Royal Navy ships.
However, today very little hemp is cultivated in the UK even though it is easy
to grow, with low financial, chemical and labour inputs (and EU subsidies) – all
of which suggest that it could be at the cornerstone of a local fibre economy
in the UK. The reasons for hemp's minority status are partly to do with its
market (traditionally heavyweight fabrics like denim) having been completely
overwhelmed by cotton and synthetic fabrics, and partly due to its link to
Cannabis sativa, the cultivation of which is illegal in many parts of the world
(see Chapter 1). Yet the main obstacle to successfully developing UK hemp
textiles is the process of mechanically harvesting and processing the fibre so
as to produce a high quality product. BioRegional has carried out a number

◄ Jacket made
from 100
per cent
hemp grown
in England
from fibre
grown and
processed by
Bioregional
and designed
by Katherine
Hamnett

of practical trials that resulted in the production of the first UK-grown pure hemp fabric for generations and found that new harvesting technology is needed to produce fibre of the right quality and price (hand processing, while producing high-quality fibre, makes fabric too expensive). It is now working with industry and farmers to test new processing methods (chiefly retting with enzymes) that reduce the economic risk and pollution potential of traditional fibre extraction techniques.

Another cornerstone of the UK's local fibre economy is wool – and it is one of the few fibres that can still be grown, scoured, spun and woven within the shores of the UK. A small farm and mill on the Isle of Mull off the west coast of Scotland has developed the Ardalanish[24] range of organic tweeds, which combine tradition, community and local resources in a beautiful, distinctive and high-quality fabric. The fibre for the cloth, from rare-breed Hebridean sheep, comes in a range of natural colours from black to chocolate brown through to silver grey and it is carefully separated to give a variation of natural shades without dyeing. At the farm mill, in a restored cowshed, the fine Hebridean woollen yarn is woven with the natural whites and fawns of the yarn from organic Shetland sheep to make ten different tweed cloths. These have featured at the Ethical Fashion Show, Paris, and are also manufactured into blankets, shawls, scarves and a range of jackets, waistcoats and hats. Ardalanish is also a community and farming revitalization project, working with rare-breed sheep and organic farming principles to maintain biodiversity and providing a market for local sheep farmers' wool.

Local does not just have to be about materials – it can also be about celebrating local culture. Toronto-based designer Joanna Notkin,[25] for example, was asked to create a product that would celebrate her native Canada through the myth of the cabin. In response, she took the tradition of using mothballs to preserve fabrics in places like log cabins and turned it on its head, creating a line of textile products with delicate blemishes so that any additional holes added by moths would serve to enhance the beauty of the product.

Local culture was also at the centre of another project: Local,[26] part of the 5 Ways research project, which captured the essence of an area and asked you to wear it proudly on your back. Local in the case of 5 Ways meant Brick Lane, London. Brick Lane has a very special character; now the centre of London's Bangladeshi community, it has a street market, acts as a base for large numbers of designer-makers and artists and is also a thriving textile and leather area. The resulting product – a bag hand-knitted from leather scraps gathered from local workshops – evolved out of a mix of these influences.

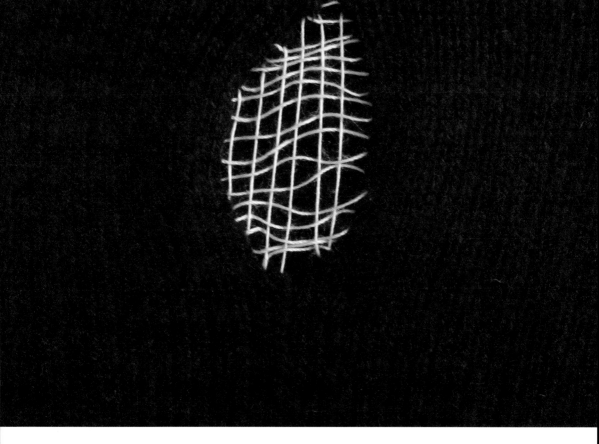

▲ Moth blanket
by Joanna
Notkin

◄ Fly skirt
in organic
tweed, part of
the Ardalanish
Collection by
Anja Hynynen
for Isle of Mull
Weavers

The leather was cut into strips, knotted into a ribbon and then knitted on chunky needles into a soft, tactile, extendable pouch. The bag is something to carry your fruit and vegetables home from the market stalls (shop local), something to indicate your community identity (this is where I live), something made from a local source of waste employing local people in the process (use waste as a resource).

Light

Designing light is a powerful way to reduce resource use without compromising function. There are lots of ways we can do this, including introducing more lightweight materials and structures and also working to maximize efficiency of products and their use. Metaphors of weight are often used when talking about taking action for sustainability; we talk about living lightly and about treading lightly on the Earth. These metaphors acknowledge that weight is a problem – that the more physical 'stuff' and the more processes we need to make something, the greater its impact – and that lightness is our challenge.[27] One key barrier to designing light is that its opposite, heaviness, has long been used as a measure of economic (and de facto societal) success. The more resources and energy we use and the more waste and pollution we emit, the more the economy grows. Perverse as it may sound, the more chemical spills or lorry journeys (with associated carbon emissions) there are, the more our society's wealth grows (as measured by the traditional indicator, gross domestic product). This is because accidents and journeys bring work for pollution clean-up and haulage companies and increase levels of economic activity. The good news is that this is changing, thanks to alternative measures of success, like the Genuine Progress Indicator, which measures well-being rather than increased production of goods. Lightness, sometimes called dematerialization, is part of this approach.

► Efficient pattern cutting concept shirt to address wastage by Andrew Hague. The basic shirt pattern is manipulated to fill the entire fabric, affecting the proportions of the new garment and its design

Lightweight materials and structures

Lightness aims to give us the same function but with lower environmental impact. Lightweight materials such as polyester and other synthetics need fewer kilograms to make more garments – reducing energy and resource consumption compared to heavier weight fabrics. Such lightweight, low-bulk fabrics are also more efficient to transport and can bring energy savings in other lifecycle phases, like consumer use. Fibres like polyester and nylon, for example, launder well on low temperatures and dry quickly with few creases – offering significant potential savings (see Chapter 3 – Use Matters). Using synthetic fibres as a low-impact solution highlights an important point: while light design is inspired by nature, it may not always use natural materials. Indeed this same, and to some people counter-intuitive, point – of natural not always being the most sustainable choice – runs through the sustainable fashion and textile design debate more generally. It is a reminder that change comes by pushing in directions that are not just familiar or conventional; it is most likely to happen when we see both the big picture and the smallest details at the same time. Typifying this complexity, designing light does not bring uncomplicated benefits. Many of the lightest and strongest materials are composites, like technical sportswear fabrics for example, which, while delivering superior function fulfilment with minimal materials, are very difficult to reuse or recycle and do not biodegrade. Our job is to work out whether such innovations contribute more to the overall system (less materials, efficient laundering) than they take out (adding to landfill) and explore alternatives where they exist.

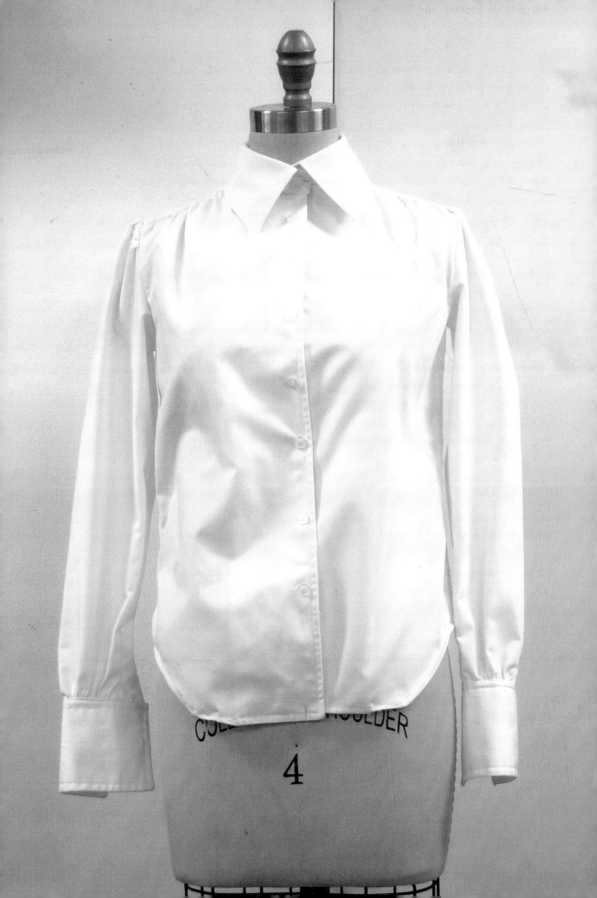

Designing light is not just about materials but also construction. Innovative hexagonal, waffle and honeycomb structures enclose the maximum amount of space with the minimum amount of materials and so give us more cover, warmth and strength for fewer kilograms. Likewise the age-old string vest, when worn in combination with other layers, is a classic example of warmth with minimal materials. Designing light through construction opens up a rich opportunity for innovation in knit and weave – and also in efficient pattern cutting; changing the proportions of a garment or the number of pattern pieces, to maximize use of fabric, uses lightness to save resources by altering garment construction.

Lightness can also be achieved by multifunction. By designing and developing one product that performs many functions, the overall effect is that we can do more with less. The Cambia T-shirt made by Páramo[28] for example, has two fabric faces and can be reversed depending on whether you need to keep cool or warm. When the smooth side is worn next to the skin, moisture is kept near the body and helps with cooling. If it is turned inside out the function of the fabric changes and the honeycomb structure directs water away from the body and keeps the wearer drier and warmer. Lightness, however, does not give the go-ahead for the development of a rash of over-designed multifunctional garments. Instead, it is about the constant adapting and reassessing of material use.

Negademand

A key part of the lightness agenda involves using products more efficiently. This lets us break the link between increasing wealth (economic activity) and the production of goods – while still meeting people's needs. What this means in practice is still relatively unexplored in the fashion and textile sector, although other industries have been developing efficient use ideas for over a decade by changing conventional business relationships in a way that improves business and resource efficiency. Utility companies, for example, have realized that helping consumers to use energy more efficiently, so reducing demand, can be good for their business. While at face value this seems to make no sense, as electricity companies' profits are linked to selling more units of power, these companies now recognize that if they persuade their customers to save energy (switch off lights, install insulation, etc.), then profits increase by not having to invest in and build more power stations, substations, electricity cables and pylons to meet growing demand. Here both supplier and customer profit from working collaboratively to eliminate wasteful consumption. This idea, termed negademand (negative demand), is central to designing light. Negademand works for corporates because they also diversify their business activity. No longer do electricity companies just sell power, they also own businesses that advise on energy efficiency, that produce energy-efficient light bulbs and fridges and install insulation in people's homes.

Negademand switches the onus away from selling products to selling efficiency. In fashion and textiles, negademand would mean that companies would sell fewer fibres, but make their money by developing businesses around forging partnerships with customers that make the use of fibres more efficient. So for example, a high street store would employ fashion stylists to advise paying customers on how to 'stretch' a wardrobe and maximize 'on trend' wearing potential of each piece and how to update existing pieces to keep them current. Other possibilities include diversifying into accessories to encourage consumers to express trend awareness in other ways. Companies could also site repair facilities in-store and even provide paid, supervised access to sewing machines, transfer presses and digital printers to encourage repair, reuse and customization. They could also branch out into web publications and style blogs – providing us with the opportunity to consume immaterial fashion imagery and information, rather than material products.

Sharing

Another key way to use products more efficiently is to share them, and then one item meets many people's needs. While many of us may already share clothes, borrowing clothes from our friends, housemates and parents, few of our garments are designed explicitly to be shared. To make garments easy to share, they have to be adaptable enough to fit a range of body sizes and shapes, perhaps making use of tapes and ties to help adjust to fit or developing pieces with as few tight fitting points as possible. This latter approach of designing unisize – and even unisex – garments with minimal fitting points so as to maximize their shareability can be seen in the work of Amy Twigger Holroyd's innovative knitwear label, Keep and Share.[29] Typical Keep and Share garments are items like shrugs, wraps and cardigans, based on loose geometric shapes and seamless finishes. Versatility of product is also matched by a versatile purchasing choice: garments are also available on loan.

◀ JP Donleavy
shrug, Spring/
Summer
2005, 100 per
cent cotton
by Keep and
Share

Services

Switching from selling products to selling the use of products through services has considerable sustainability potential – offering around a factor 10 (i.e. 90 per cent) improvement in efficiency.[30] Services provide opportunities to meet needs with fewer resources and less energy (i.e. lighter) because they are focused on utility or results and not strictly on materials. The core concept is that, as consumers, we seek not the product (say for example, towels), but rather the functionality that it offers us (dry hands). Moreover, if business can be structured to encourage this shift in focus, then we can perhaps begin to meet needs with fewer physical goods, which in turn leads to fewer environmental impacts. The opportunities to reduce impact flow from designers being able to think about customer needs in new ways. No longer limited by their traditional view of what they must deliver to the customer (continuing the example above – cotton hand towels), designers can develop the best solution to meet the customer's need (paper towels, hot air dryers, etc.). This in itself is a challenge as the 'best' solution may well fall outside traditional industry boundaries and so be difficult to achieve unless sustainability initiatives work in trans-industrial groups. Real gains are also dependent on using designers' expert knowledge of consumption and knowledge of how to make products desirable for the service sector. As Chris Ryan notes,

> …market success depends on the way (cultural and social) meanings are materialized and projected onto a product… Designers are skilled in manipulating material form to create products that function to fulfill human needs and make an emotional connection with the consumer. If there is to be a replacement of products by services, these new systems will have to be designed to be more desirable than material goods for consumers.[31]

It is important to stress that a shift towards a service economy is not necessarily a shift towards sustainability. In the information-rich, knowledge-based service economy of the first decade of the 21st century – the service sector makes up almost 70 per cent of the European economy[32] – consumption has increased, not reduced. So services are not better for the environment per se; they have to be so by design. For example, in the case of garments, the most environmentally damaging phase of the lifecycle is use or laundering. Sharing a garment with multiple users has little effect on how it is washed and dried – meaning that switching to a service effectively chases the wrong goal (see Chapter 3 – Use Matters). Yet services might be the right solution for other textile products, like carpets or furnishings say, where most impact is amassed in production.

There are a number of commercially viable businesses that offer fashion and textile services, though very few of them are examples of 'transformed systems' – businesses that use services proactively to promote sustainability. Perhaps the best-known 'transformed' business that uses services in the fashion and textile sector is American carpet company Interface and its Evergreen Lease carpet rental system.[33] Evergreen Lease sells customers underfoot colour, comfort and warmth by leasing carpet tiles. Under the lease arrangement, the tiles remain the property of Interface and when worn are removed and returned to its factory for closed-loop materials recycling, which aims to reduce the amount of virgin material used and the amount of end-of-life material being disposed of in landfills or by incineration. Evergreen Lease makes money by designing tiles to last, so that replacement costs are kept to a minimum, and adds value through ease of recycling – reclaiming and reusing the valuable raw materials in a worn carpet. The system is attractive to consumers because it saves money, Evergreen Lease is priced cheaper than the bought equivalent over the lifetime of a carpet and, in addition, companies no longer have to buy a carpet outright, so taking a significant cost off the balance sheet. Yet disappointingly, Evergreen Lease has not brought huge business or environmental benefits to Interface, chiefly because of cultural issues and resistance to new ways of being supplied with products.

Research carried out by Marcus Wong[34] at the University of Cambridge investigated the barriers to the successful introduction of Evergreen Lease. These include, among others:

- the complexity of selling services – involving more people than for selling products, an understanding of more detailed contracts, and a better knowledge of the customer organization;
- the customer's education – customers need to have a long-term view of their organization to see the benefits of the service and know how to communicate this to the different budget holders involved;
- the resistance to change – if customers fail to see a problem with their existing solution, there is a very low level of motivation to change and an accompanying high level of scepticism about the alternative.

The experience of Evergreen Lease highlights the innate difficulties of introducing sustainable services into a market traditionally dominated by the selling of products. However, other companies have carved out a successful service niche in the existing market and provide, for instance, formal or evening wear hire, lease of maternity clothes or linen hire. In the case of formal wear like suits, evening dresses and wedding outfits, hiring allows consumers to wear an expensive garment that is going to be worn as a one-off without buying it outright – advantages enjoyed by celebrities when they 'borrow' gowns for red-carpet gala events. For maternity wear, rapidly changing body shape means that the garment (particularly something like office or formal wear for professional women) is only going to be worn for a short period before it no longer fits. Hiring can allow women to get appropriate-sized or special-occasion maternity clothes more cheaply. In the case of textile or linen rental, uniforms, bed or hospitality linen for the catering industry, services can loan just the products or also offer laundry and dry cleaning facilities, saving companies time and capital expense of buying and running cleaning equipment.

Thus leasing can make a profit for both retailer and consumer. What is more, a recent research project investigating this area[35] suggests that a system of leasing clothing could bring substantial environmental benefits, saving water, energy and chemicals and reducing the amount of garments being sent to landfill. Importantly, the project also recognized that leased clothing would only be possible under certain conditions and if social and cultural changes took place, including a change in consumer attitudes and behaviour towards environmental issues. Also needed would be substantial changes from retailers, redesigning their manufacturing expertise to also include repair, changing the layout of their stores and buying laundry equipment. In favour of a shift to leased clothing are new business practices like just-in-time manufacturing, where high street retailers respond to changing trends not just in seasonal collections but by bringing new garments in store every two weeks (see Chapter 2 – Ethically Made). So-called fast fashion and the availability of 'value' clothes has led to rapidly increasing rates of consumption and has changed our relationship with clothes. Fast-to-consume clothes are more throwaway, less cherished and less personal – something that may indicate consumers' readiness to lease, not own, garments in order to utilize their material and symbolic functions.

The collection of projects, companies and ideas introduced in this chapter all help support a wealth of differentiated and more sustainable activity. Indeed many of these projects simultaneously influence sustainability in all of its three domains: society/culture, environment and economy. Yet for these alternatives to bring big change and become widely adopted, they also have to be experientially and physically beautiful. After all, it is the prestige and high levels of cultural attractiveness of alternatives that is central to a smooth transition to sustainability.[36]

CHAPTER SEVEN Speed

Fast fashion has become a defining characteristic of today's textile and cloth-ing industry. It is a combination of high speed production – tracking sales with electronic tills, and just-in-time manufacturing that now makes it possible to turn a sample or design sketch into a finished product in as little as three weeks – and high speed, high volume consumption. A recent report revealed that people are buying one third more garments than four years ago,[1] fuelled by the rise of cheap clothes and 'value' retailers like Primark and Matalan. Yet super-cheap, 'value' or 'fast fashion' garments are no quicker to make or consume than any other garment. The fibre takes the same amount of time to grow regardless of a product's speed to market (in the case of cotton, around eight months to cultivate and two to ship). Likewise the raw material takes the same amount of time to be spun, knitted or woven, cleaned, bleached, dyed, printed, cut and sewn; and the activity of going shopping and laundering the garment takes the same amount of time regardless of how speedily a design makes it from studio to high street retailer.

'Fast' in the case of today's fashion industry describes economic speed. Time is one of the factors of production, along with labour, capital and natural resources, that get juggled and squeezed in the pursuit of maximizing throughput of goods for increased profits. But increasing the speed of pro-duction and consumption comes at a cost. Rapidly changing style and novelty is workable only because clothing is so cheap (indeed, over the last 15 years the price of garments has been falling), made possible by the shifting of pro-duction to low-cost countries, and by putting downward pressure on working conditions and environmental standards, the so-called 'race to the bottom'.

But there are other views of time and speed, which acknowledge not just economic speed but also nature's speed and the pace of change of culture. These other views give us a key portal into the designing and making of more ecological, user-centred and resourceful fabrics and garments. These views provide us with a multilayered focus on speed that is a marked shift in emphasis away from the status quo in today's industry where fashion is mass-produced and textiles are consumed en masse. They are part of a different world-view, where a sensitivity to speed in both production and consumption is transformed into a force for quality (of environment, society, pay, working conditions and products, etc.). Its aim is to reframe the use of speed as a force for sustainability and not just as a vehicle for promoting discontinu-ity (by introducing contrasting styles each collection), consumption (as we replace old styles with new) and wealth (almost exclusively for the fashion industry elite).

This chapter examines the potential for using ideas of speed to promote environmental and social quality, and investigates the ideas and practice of designing fabrics and garments with different and carefully selected speed and rhythms of use. Speed can be both fast and slow (and an infinite variety of other paces). Fast actions innovate and can bring rapid feedback and speedy take-up of improved products. Slowness provides stability and can promote holistic thinking and causal chains of responsibility. Combining the two brings newness underpinned by resilience, revolution bolstered by remembrance, and fashion supported by nature and culture.

Speed and rhythms in nature and culture

Applying ideas of speed and rhythms of use to fashion and textiles helps us develop a new vision for the sector that has the potential to reduce some of the negative impacts of consumerist 'fast' fashion. If we look at how speed is dealt with in nature we see combinations of fast and slow. Ecosystems achieve balance and long-term resilience of the larger system by adjusting to change at different paces. Nature typically combines change that happens on a big scale but very slowly (like the time needed to grow a mature, established forest) with fast, small-scale change (such as in the lifecycle of a flowering plant). Here the varying rates of change within the ecosystem effectively help sustain it, allowing it to survive potentially damaging events. This is because the fast parts react while the slower parts maintain system continuity.[2]

This same sense of combining different speeds can be seen in the views of time of many indigenous and ancient cultures. The ancient Greeks, for example, talked of two different kinds of time, *kairos* (opportunity or the propitious moment), and *chronos* (eternal or ongoing time). Building on both this cultural legacy and nature's use of speed, Stewart Brand[3] proposes that any resilient human civilization needs similar layers of fast and slow activity to balance each other. He suggests six levels of pace and size (see Figure 7.1), noting that when the whole system is balanced, it 'combines learning with continuity'. From fast to slow (and of increasing size) the layers are: Art/fashion, Commerce, Infrastructure, Governance, Culture and Nature. The fastest layers, like fashion, bring rapid imaginative change, while the slowest layers maintain constancy and provide long-term supporting structure. Crucially, the system works when each layer respects the pace of the others.

Yet the fashion industry, as it exists today, has no respect for these other

Figure 7.1 *Layers of activity in a resilient human civilization*

layers. Indeed a growing body of evidence suggests that it is largely disconnected from the effects of its products on nature and culture, with little recognition of poverty wages, forced overtime, waste mountains and climate change. In fact the commercial agenda in fashion seems to promote the polar opposite of a multilayered, multispeed industry. Instead what is marketed to consumers is a wide range of similar products. Making similar, generic products is of course much faster than bespoke items. Economic speed pushes us towards a one-size-fits-all culture and a herd mentality among designers. It produces products that are clones of each other and obscures long term perspectives (see Chapter 8 – User Maker). In order to promote an industry that is resilient over the long term, we need, following Brand's suggestion, to strike a balance of different speeds and agendas. This could give a voice to nature, society and culture in our design and production decisions and build a more user-centred, heterogeneous and resourceful fabrics and garments industry.

Thus the challenge of sustainability is to connect the fashion and textile industry with multiple layers of other human activity. In this way we will continue to make money, while respecting the rights of workers and the environment at the same time as meeting our requirements for newness and change as expressed through our garments. Ideas of speed can help us do this. To apply the lens of speed to fashion and textiles, there are a number of key ideas that are useful to understand, including user behaviour, appropriateness and durability. They involve industry and consumers and relate not only to how long materials last, but also to how long we keep them and how we launder them. Design has potential to influence both groups and affect change in all of these areas, working both to shape products and to facilitate new types of behaviour. In effect the ideas of speed have at their essence celebration: celebration of the glorious bits of fashion (a fast layer, dealing with newness, change and fashion symbolism) and of really good making and material quality (a slow layer, dealing with resourcefulness and optimization). It requires us to find ways to extend the value and use of some products while simultaneously learning how to express the fashion moment while minimizing the impact of material consumption.

Durability

Durability is a key component of any exploration of speed in design. It is also a popular strategy and represents long-established 'good' design qualities like efficiency and timelessness. Durability is often seen as a truly sustainable approach, an antidote to fashion change. Moreover, extending the life of products does bring benefits; resources are saved because fewer units are consumed to meet the same needs. According to Tim Cooper,[4] a long-term advocate of durable products, environmental benefits are accrued from extending product life (of all products – not just textiles and clothing) in all but the most extreme cases in which technological change brings greatly improved efficiency. As such, designing for durability appears to be a legitimate design and production activity in a world already choked with products, where consumers buy more than they need. Indeed in some circles there have been calls for all clothes to be designed for long life, transcending time and fashion changes, and so reducing the amount we produce and consume.[5]

In practical terms, the durability of textiles and clothing can be increased in a variety of ways. One common approach is to focus on improving the physical and technical robustness of the fabric/garment so that it almost defies the ageing process. This can be done by using hard-wearing materials that are slow to show signs of wear and tear; high-quality making techniques that ensure a product keeps its shape; and avoiding the use of highly stylized prints or patterns that quickly date a product. Durable products are perhaps particularly suited to the high-end market where there is a tradition of specifying quality materials (although quality does not necessarily equate to robustness) and using highly skilled craft techniques that naturally chime with many sustainability values. Yet pursuing a blanket strategy of expensive materials and craft making is exclusive and unrealistic. Not only would demand massively outstrip supply and these objects become the preserve of the rich, but a strategy of all-embracing durability also fails to appreciate the centrality of fashion to human culture and the reasons why we buy and throw away as we do.

Not all things are thrown away just because they are worn out, but rather, in most cases, because people are bored with them. Evidence from two different surveys bears this out. The first, a study of Scandinavian consumers, shows that new clothes are bought primarily because of a change in fashion and only very rarely to replace old, worn-out garments.[6] Thus revealing a major discrepancy between idealized notions of how long things ought to last and the starker reality of what actually happens. The second study, this time of British clothing designers, underlines this further and reveals a significant gap between the length of time designers feel materials should last ('all materials should be very durable') and the average length of time the garment stays on trend ('around six months').[7] This inconsistency perhaps shows more about the popular, aspirational nature of durability as a design strategy than insensitivity to questions of how long products last. Yet it also reinforces the point that the length of time for which a garment lasts is influenced by culture, behaviour and emotion as well as purely technical or material factors. Without this broader appreciation, a strategy of making all fabrics and garments last decades even if they are only worn once wastes resources.

▶ Eugenia dress, Spring/ Summer 2006, 100 per cent cotton by Keep and Share

Appropriateness

Thus it becomes clear that making a product last is very different to making a long-lasting product. At the core of a fabric or garment's lasting usefulness is the idea of appropriateness. Appropriateness reflects the degree of 'fit' that an object has with place, function, user, maker and environment. Ann Thorpe has described this quality as 'finesse', the 'artful restraint and delicacy of performance or behaviour … finesse means not doing everything it is possible to do. Rather, finesse means resisting the force of speed through aesthetic and sensitive behaviour.'[8] Sustaining the use of a fabric or garment into the future requires sensitivity to a number of factors that are not the usual concern of designers today. This involves knowing more about how long materials last, about how products are used, and about why products stop being used. The result should be the selection of materials appropriate to their expected lifetime's task; the development of design strategies such as versatility and reparability to keep a product relevant; the promotion of emotional bonds with a product which encourage ongoing use; and an overall sensitivity to how fabrics and garments are actually used.

Many designers and companies, some of whom work regularly with sustainability ideas, have produced pieces that exemplify appropriateness. Keep and Share,[9] for example, specializes in versatile, long life garments. Uni-size, unisex knitwear is designed with anchor points to attach to a wrist or shoulder and with loose geometric shapes that drape around the body, resulting in a garment that can be shared between people. This intensifies use and saves resources because the same piece meets a number of people's needs. As well as intensifying use, Keep and Share promotes longevity through a strong, 'love it or hate it' aesthetic with offbeat colour palettes and by establishing a community of customers linked to each other via its boutique-type website. Appropriateness can also be secured by developing repairable, upgradable products. A Barbour[10] jacket, for instance, the quintessential garment of the English countryside, can be sent away for repair and refurbishing. Restitched linings and rewaxed outer layers keep a garment functional for longer – and just like with a select few other garments (such as jeans), the more battered and worn they become, the more they are prized.

In his book *Emotionally Durable Design*, Jonathan Chapman[11] explains appropriateness as a function of a product's emotional presence, evolution and growth. He suggests that it is not enough for a product to provoke an emotional response in the user on one occasion; it must do this repeatedly. In effect a relationship must be developed between user and object over an extended period of time. Exploring these ideas, Sigrid Smits[12] developed a furnishing fabric as part of the noteworthy Eternally Yours project,[13] specifically designed to age with the user. Growing old with a fabric (perhaps upholstered on a chair), witnessing it change over time and in response to the user's actions and behaviour, is fertile ground from which emotional attachment and long-term product use springs. Smits' blue velour furnishing fabric was pleated, tucked and shorn, to enhance (not resist) ageing and to further emphasize unique and beautiful qualities that spring from user engagement. As the velour ages, the orange backing fabric becomes more visible, especially in stitched or shorn areas, and helps mark the passing of time.

Small acts can begin to trigger meaning and emotional connections. Such things as an oversized label that comes with an invitation for a user to sign it as a piece of 'future archeology' (like those in Hussein Chalayan's ready-to-wear collection) can connect a person with a garment and reinforce a bond of ownership. But more than that, signing a garment as you would a contract can also be seen as declaration of responsibility and expression of long-term commitment. This act can help bring to the surface the relationships we have with our clothes. One aspect of a recent project by Otto von Busch[14] explored some of these ideas further. He set up a small temporary shop stocked with clothes. While none of the garments could be bought with money, they could, however, be 'bought' by swapping them for what the 'customer' was wearing that day. To make the exchange, the customer had to first write down their feelings about their garment, why they no longer liked it and why they had originally bought it. The simple act of thinking about their garment and articulating their emotions and preferences about the piece meant that most people changed their minds about the swap and elected instead to keep the piece they were wearing. So while value and meaning are influenced by a complex mix of factors, it seems that they can be triggered in simple ways. Learning to trigger meaning in clothes could for example add reuse value and cachet to second-hand pieces, possibly increasing the likelihood of a second life (see Chapter 4 – Reuse, Recycling and Zero Waste).

Yet even if materials are not the chief factor influencing an object's sustainability, they still play an important role. Resources can be saved by matching quality of materials to utilization time so that physical durability is extended only when it is needed. To do this effectively we need to know more about

▷ Blue velour pleated furnishing fabric by Sigrid Smits

the energy and resources that go into making fabrics (see Chapter 1); recycling loops and composting of materials (see Chapter 4); and patterns of use,
which are explored in more detail below.

Understanding patterns of use

Understanding how and for how long fabrics and garments are used and
maintained is central to using ideas of speed to build a more sustainable industry. This helps us distinguish between pieces that are consumed as quick,
immaterial fashion 'hits' and others which are bought for more functional, material reasons. In recognizing these differences we raise the prospect of designing, in parallel, a number of different and more resource-efficient rhythms
and speeds of consumption for different textile products. In the case of
furnishings, designing to enhance durability and a 'slow' rhythm of use would
probably bring resource benefits. For clothing, however, the picture is more

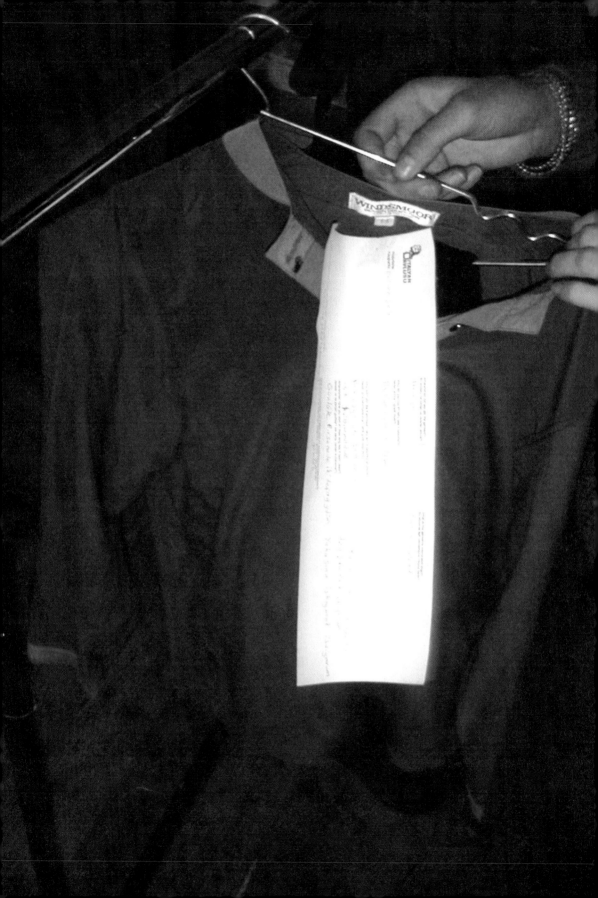

◀ Oversized
labels and
clothes rails in
Itaylan Avlusu
project swap
'shop' set up
by Otto von
Busch

involved because of the relative importance of laundering behaviour in determining overall lifecycle impact and because not all types of clothing are worn
and washed in the same way. For those garments that are rarely washed and
which are worn for years, slow rhythms of use (and related design strategies
supporting both physical and emotional durability) are likely to bring most
benefits. Yet for long haul, frequently washed garments, substantial resource
savings are more likely to be achieved by targeting the impacts arising from
the use phase. Speculatively, this might mean that designers focus on changing people's laundering habits (see Chapter 3 – Use Matters) or introducing
fast rhythms of use, where garments are disposed of before laundering.

To further illustrate how patterns of use can affect lifecycle impacts of
clothing, Figure 7.2 shows energy data from Franklin Associates' LCA of
a woman's polyester blouse (see Chapter 3 for a discussion of this study)
extrapolated for five different use scenarios. The base case used in this study
assumes that the blouse is worn 40 times in its life and is laundered after
every other wearing (i.e. 20 times). The other scenarios are: long life, where
the blouse is worn for twice as long as in the base case (i.e. 80 times) and like
the base case is laundered after every second wearing; low wash, where the
blouse is worn 40 times (as in the base case) but is washed half as often (after
every four wearings); disposable 1, where the blouse is worn five times, then
discarded and never laundered; and disposable 2, where the blouse is worn
ten times, then thrown away without washing.

While it is important not to over-interpret the results of these scenarios, as
they only show energy use and therefore don't give a complete picture, they
do illustrate the extent to which use patterns can influence a garment's overall
energy profile and in which lifecycle phase the majority of impact arises. For

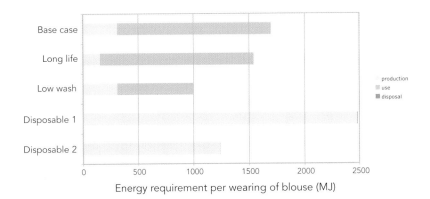

Figure 7.2 *Energy requirements per wearing of a polyester blouse for a range of use
scenarios*[15]

the two disposable scenarios, the energy burden is almost exclusively in the production phase – the implication here is that more efficient production processes or different materials could radically cut lifecycle energy use. While for the other three scenarios, impact arising from laundering is the biggest factor – so targeting this high-impact phase would probably bring the biggest gains. Above all, the results reiterate the point that for frequently washed clothes the biggest resource savings come from influencing use patterns.

One way to influence use patterns is to design garments for short lives and no laundering, in effect designing for disposability. Disposability is a loaded concept in sustainability terms as it is readily associated with profligate resource use and disposal. Yet for products where the cost of upkeep is high relative to the cost of production – like frequently washed clothes – carefully designed short-life garments may save resources overall. Yet to make short-life products a viable and more sustainable alternative, innovation in materials and material recovery is essential. Low-impact short-life products would have to be made from materials of a quality that matched the short life. They would be resource-efficient in production and in disposal – either readily biodegradable or effectively recycled without losing quality (see Chapter 4) and only then could they be seen to offer a real alternative for certain products.

The divisions between fashion and clothes (described in Chapter 5) seem to naturally emphasize different lengths of life and rhythms of use. Fashion pieces are 'consumed' at a quicker rate than non-fashion clothes – they are 'in' right now and usually connected to certain colours and styles, they have high symbolism and are worn visibly ('on show') for communication with others, and when the symbols change, the garment is discarded. In contrast, non-fashion items tend to be consumed at a slower pace. The motive behind purchasing and wearing these garments is both material functionality and stylishness. The remainder of this chapter explores a more sustainable and speed-inspired vision for fashion and textiles.

Slow design

At the core of sustainability is a requirement that we make our systems of wealth creation less dependent on resource use. One way to do this is re-evaluate our relationship with speed – and normally to slow it down. John Thackara,[16] for instance, suggests that the cultural paradigm of speed is in decline and recommends instead a culture built around a greater variety of speeds and 'selective slowness'. Continuing this theme, Manzini and Jégou[17] describe a shift away from today's (unsustainable) product-based society to a new culture where community assets are valued more highly and where we develop 'islands of slowness'. Ideas of slow design, production and consumption were first developed in the Slow Food Movement. Founded by Carlo Petrini in Italy in 1986, Slow Food links pleasure and food with awareness and responsibility. It seeks to defend biodiversity in our food supply, by opposing the standardization of taste, defending the need for consumer information and protecting cultural identities tied to food. It has spawned a wealth of other slow movements. Slow Cities, for example, design with slow values but within the context of a town or city, and are committed to improving the quality of life of its citizens. Slow Food makers, along with artisan producers and farmers markets, have experienced rapid growth in recent years, establishing slow as a viable alternative to our current culture. The Slow Food Movement provides us with ample evidence that people are prepared to pay for what is scarce, customized and carefully made – a finding that is likely to be at least partly applicable to the fashion sector.

Slow fashion

In melding the slow movement's ideas with the global clothing industry, we build a new vision for fashion in the era of sustainability: where pleasure and fashion is linked with awareness and responsibility. This both affirms the importance of fashion to our culture and recognizes the urgency of the sustainability agenda. Slow fashion is about designing, producing, consuming and living better. It is about combining ideas about a sense of nature's time (of regenerating cycles and evolution), culture's time (of the value of traditions and wisdom), as well as the more common timeframes of fashion and commerce. Its emphasis is on quality (of environment, society, working conditions, business, product, etc.). So slow in this context is not the opposite of fast – there is no dualism – it is simply a different approach in which designers, buyers, retailers and consumers are more aware of the impacts of products on workers, communities and ecosystems.

The heightened awareness of other stakeholders and speeds in slow fashion along with the emphasis on quality gives rise to different relationships between designer and maker; maker and garment; garment and user. Recognizing and designing with speeds other than just a fast commercial pace takes the pressure off time. Garments are still mass-produced, but they are done so in supplier factories that pay living wages and maintain high standards. Mutually beneficial relationships between retailers, top brands and their suppliers are fostered over the longer term. This helps erase the unpredictability for suppliers of small volume orders and short lead times, which frequently lead to the use of temporary workers and forced overtime that has become the hallmark of today's consumerist fashion.

At the heart of the idea of slow fashion is balance. In Brand's vision of a more resilient human civilization described earlier (see Figure 7.1), newness and innovation are represented, as is long-term stability. Accordingly, slow fashion combines these layers and includes products that are designed for rapid imaginative change and symbolic (fashion) expression as well as those designed for material durability and emotional engagement. Only in balancing these speeds and rhythms of use will quality be achieved. Quality normally comes at a price and at least some slow fashion pieces will cost substantially more than they do today, reflecting their materials, workmanship and values. This will result in us buying fewer high-value, slow-to-consume products and bring key resource savings. It has been suggested for example that the sector could halve its materials use without economic loss if consumers pay a higher price for a product that lasts twice as long.[18] Yet other slow fashion pieces may cost the same or even less than today. These will be specifically designed to be resource-efficient, quick-to-consume products developed, say, as part of carefully planned materials cycles.

Designing for this multilayered, diverse, quality-based agenda is our next challenge. Janine Benyus' book *Biomimicry* offers us one possible starting point. She provides a series of descriptors of ecosystems in both their developing stages (where fast proliferating species predominate) and mature stages (where slow species prevail) (see Table 7.1).[19] This gives us some clues as to how nature has evolved these different speeds as part of the process of ecological succession. Fast species tend to be small, simple and quick to break down. Slow species are complex, robust and long-lasting. Designing with these differences can help us develop a more sustainable and multilayered approach to designing fashion and textiles.

Table 7.1 *Characteristics of ecosystems in different stages of evolution*

Developing stages (fast species)	Mature stages (slow species)
Small body size	Large body size
Low species diversity	High species diversity
Short, simple lifecycle	Long, complex lifecycle
Production - quantity	Production - quality
Pattern diversity - simple	Pattern diversity - complex
Stability/resilience - poor	Stability/resilience - good

This idea of slow fashion tied to rhythms of use was first developed in the Lifetimes project, described in more detail below.

The Lifetimes project

The Lifetimes project[20] was a small research project focused on exploring the potential for designing more sustainable textile products by being more sensitive to users and ideas of time. Its aim was to develop a more sustainable and more complex model of clothing design, where account was taken of use patterns, fashion levels and how long things last. This involved finding ways to extend the value of some products (by looking at the emotional durability of long-lasting clothes) and to find ways to express fashion, change and communication with minimal consumption (by looking to new types of materials, new cycles of use and service opportunities). Critical to the project was the notion of balance. Just as in ecosystems where fast change and renewal is complemented by slowness and stability, balance would also need to be achieved in the speed of consumption of fabrics and garments. Otherwise there would be no net reduction in consumption.

One of the project's outcomes was a series of design scenarios that offered a vision of the future based around new rhythms of consumption, dictated by us and not the system. Design scenarios are an important part of the development of different and more resourceful ways of producing textile products. They can also be relevant to today's world – by working with what is already available they can reveal multiple opportunities for fashion and textile designers to innovate around the theme of sustainability. The scenarios of fast and slow clothes were concerned with saving resources while simultaneously providing for people's symbolic (fashion) and material (clothing) needs. By designing garments with fast and slow rhythms of use, transience and durability can both be celebrated but within a holistic, sustainable value system concerned with efficiency, balance and quality of life. Fast and slow clothes are specific and never generic, and as such this project worked with named garments. For each of four garments, data was gathered about their resource consumption and patterns of use, through user diaries and wardrobe inventories. This informed the building of scenarios, the aim of which was to inspire the design of new more user- and resource-sensitive garments. The four garments were: a party top, basic underwear, utility trousers and a plain coat. They were chosen because they reflect short- and long-life pieces, a variety of laundering profiles, and because they meet needs in a range of ways. This chapter concludes with these scenarios.

Party top

The party top is an impulse buy. Feeling good, buying something for a specific occasion and being 'in' are the primary motives for its purchase. The top's fashion level is high and it is worn a number of times for a short period and then relegated to the back of the wardrobe.

The assumption is that the top is made from polyester and because it's worn for such a limited time, and may never be washed, the production phase of the lifecycle has the highest impact. Key environmental impacts of the polyester party top include:

- energy use in production of the polyester;
- emissions to air and water from polyester production that have a medium to high potential of causing environmental damage if discharged untreated, including heavy metal cobalt, manganese salts, sodium bromide and titanium dioxide;
- the cost of disposal – synthetic fabrics like polyester are non-biodegradable and while they can be effectively recycled, most are currently sent to landfill.

Design scenario: One-night wonder

One night a glamour queen, another a fashion butterfly. Short-wear party tops have short lives, like the paper dresses of the 1960s and experimental wedding dresses of today. These garments have a low-impact production profile, fastidiously avoiding the use of virgin materials and keeping the amount of material in the garment to a minimum. They are either completely biodegradable or highly recyclable and are 'taken back' by producers from consumers. The cost of recycling or composting is included in the price and a deposit paid back to the customer when she returns the garment. New trends emerge around themes of temporary beauty and ornate yet transient garments.

In contrast to the ultra-disposable party top, the one-night wonder is also the ultra-covetable vintage piece and is perfect to rent, as it's desired for reasons of 'fashion' and 'occasion' and not for sentimental value. Just as celebrities borrow designer gowns or jewellery for film premieres, 'ordinary' people rent a desired garment for a specific time. The rental shop is organized like a high street shop and takes influences from lifestyle concepts such as Colette, Paris or vintage shops, thus answering the growing trend for one-offs and individual choice.

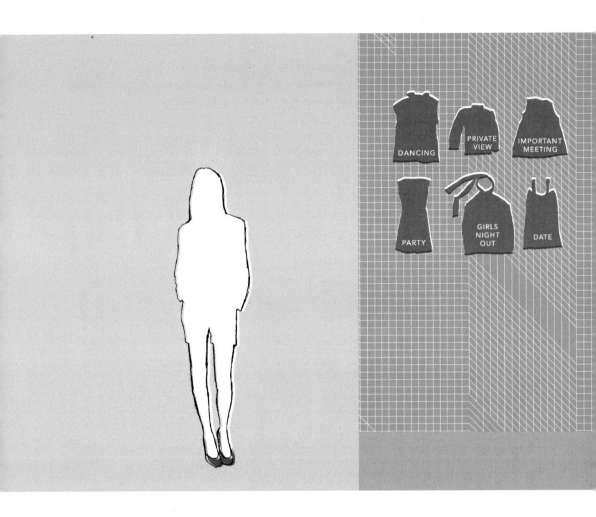

Basic underwear has a low fashion level and is bought because it provides comfort at a good price. Therefore it works almost exclusively at the biological, material level (i.e. for warmth and protection). Underwear typically has a long, regular use and is laundered very frequently.

It is assumed that the underwear is made from a cotton/nylon mix and as a result of its frequent washing, the consumer care stage of the lifecycle has most impact. Key environmental impacts of the mixed-fibre basic underwear include:

- the consumption of large amounts of energy, water and detergent in laundering;
- emissions to air, water and land arising from laundering.

Design scenario: Fancy pants

Above all, comfortable, basic underwear screens other garments from bodily dirt and smells and acts as the sacrificial layer that is washed often and changed daily. Underwear is either disposable or designed for low-impact laundering. Disposable knickers are not ugly NHS-surplus, but are soft, delicate and lacy, laser-cut to precision. They are made from a low-impact fabric (such as a non-woven cellulose) and are coloured only with readily and safely biodegradable pigments. They are supplied in bulk and come complete with composting instructions to rapidly transform your undergarments, along with vegetable peelings, into garden mulch.

Low-impact laundering for the non-disposables takes the form of advice on spot cleaning, 'freshening up', correct dosing of detergents and how long to leave clothes in the washing basket before washing to facilitate stain and smell removal. This advice comes neatly interwoven with the design of the underwear in the form of storage bags, ribbons and labels, one not complete without the other.

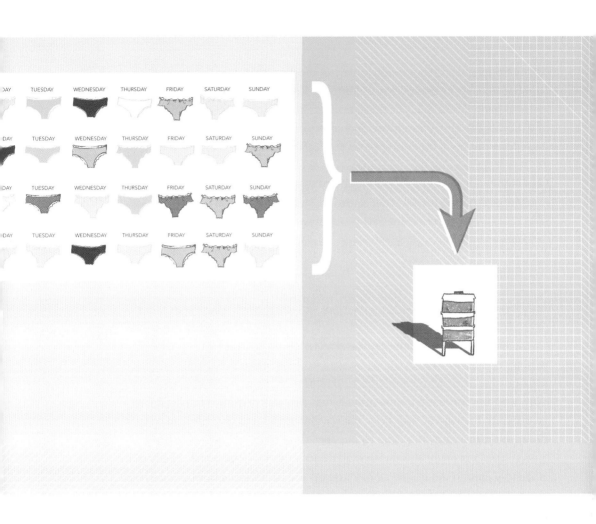

Utility trousers

▷ Who wears
the trousers?

Utility trousers occur in a variety of styles, most frequently in the form of combat trousers or denim jeans. Combats, like jeans, can be bought new or second-hand. Since many of these trousers are bought ready customized, it is the individual's ability to choose and style well, rather than the brand or price tag of the garment, that determines the fashion level.

It is assumed that the utility trousers are made from cotton and are washed and dried regularly (although not every wearing). The use phase of the lifecycle generates substantial environmental impact; however, production costs are also important. Key environmental impacts of cotton utility trousers include:

- impacts of industrial-scale cotton growing, including use of toxic chemicals (pesticides) and major water consumption;
- the consumption of large amounts of energy, water and detergent in laundering;
- emissions to air, water and land arising from laundering.

Design scenario: Who wears the trousers?
New trousers are made from materials that age well and have the flexibility to adapt to the wearer over time. Rather than designing this garment to look 'worn' or 'distressed', this is up to the user. Over time, her own pain (they need to be broken in) along with marks and scuffs build up a web of affection and story around the trousers which means she wants to keep wearing them.

But if she wants to buy them ready 'worn', then she buys second-hand. Several high street brands such as H&M and Top Shop already offer second-hand clothes in-store and this would be rolled out across the high street. This drags the charity shop treasures out of smelly jumble sales and into mainstream stores to be mixed and matched more freely with new items. This is accompanied by a high street patching service that smartens, cleans up and extends the life of these 'friends'.

Stories are a big part of the trousers' past and future. They remind her of a night out in Berlin/eating chips on Brighton Pier. The story also promotes low-impact maintenance. A detailed, yet easy-to-follow set of instructions printed on deliciously tactile labels in the pockets remind you to wash on low temperatures and 'freshen-up' in a steamy room.

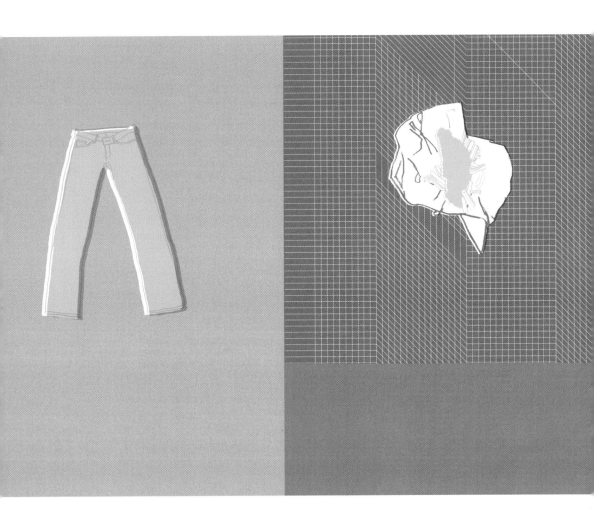

The plain coat is the archetypical slow garment; it is generally bought only after due thought and consideration (although to what degree, is determined by its price). The motives behind its purchase are both material functionality and stylishness. Even those brands with a high fashion level tend to design coats for the medium to long term. The coat is used intensively for some periods of the year and is dry-cleaned once a season. It is stored carefully in between times.

The assumption is that the coat is made from 100 per cent wool and, because it is never/rarely cleaned, the main environmental impact is in the production phase of the lifecycle. Key environmental impacts of a plain woollen coat include:

-       pesticides used on sheep, that cause harm to human health and water courses both on the farm and in subsequent downstream processing;
-       effluents arising from wool scouring – which are significant in terms of their pollution potential to both water and land (in the form of wool grease sludge).

Design scenario: Great coat
The coat is produced in enduring virgin material with high quality finishing, accessories and tailoring. Rather than resisting all signs of wear and tear, the fabric ages gracefully and fits like the proverbial glove. The coat has a definite yet flexible design and comes with spare buttons, thread and swatches of fabric for mending, and an ongoing relationship with the designer/store to restyle or refit the coat. The fashion company offers new accessories according to trends, updating the coat through the seasons. Other slow coats are designed as modular systems where parts are acquired and discharged according to the customer's desire.

The coat comes with meticulous instructions for maintenance attached, well-designed labels and packaging, a history of its origin including who designed it, where and what the inspiration was and where it was made so as to help crystallize a life-long relationship between user and garment. Advice on how to rid the coat of 'pub smells' and how to keep it in shape, along with a storage bag, hanger and cedar block to deter moths, are designed into the coat.

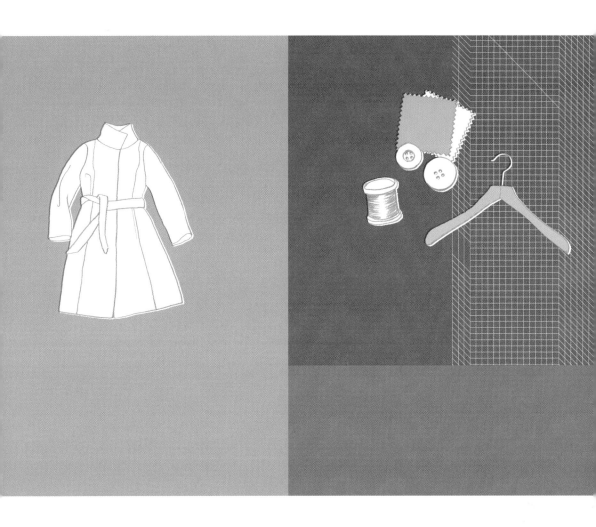

CHAPTER EIGHT User Maker

Fashion seems wedded to consumerism. Loosening this tie is at the heart of a shift to a new and more sustainable fashion and textile sector. Many of the ideas and approaches explored in this book signal the start of this unravelling. These ideas, which include slow fashion, designing with needs and development of local products among others, are types of design activism and relate less to design as a creator of things and more to design as a promoter of social change. Action and change are of central importance to sustainability, as long-term environmental and social quality requires that we develop a new model of individual and social action that is different to the one we have today. The challenge of sustainability is to learn to live better, enriching the ties that bind us together as a society and regenerating environments while also consuming much less.

This chapter looks at another form of this design activism, participatory design (sometimes called meta-design or co-design) and the potential for designing together to foster a more connected and active engagement with fashion and textiles. This type of design involves itself in a different distribution of power and inclusion than we see in most mass-produced and mass-consumed fashion and textiles today. It is concerned with a more active and skilled role for users and a system of production that is more decentralized. Accordingly, participatory design is an unabashed challenge to the hegemony of high street consumerist fashion and a stand against the dominance of elitist brands and identikit products. Its aim is to help the values of sustainability (which include appropriateness, connectedness and engagement as well as the more strictly environmental values like resourcefulness) become more embedded in our ideas of material culture, and to help change our everyday relationships with fashion and textiles.

Passive fashion

For most of us today, our everyday relationships with clothes are likely to be passive and probably a little disappointing. This passivity starts as we go shopping for clothes and continues as we wear them. Most fashion on offer in the high street is formulaic and gives consumers little choice. A recent survey of UK town centres found that almost half were virtually indistinguishable from each other, dominated by the same large chain stores that sell the same choice of products at all locations, giving the consumer the same experience (down to the sales assistants' outfits).[1] Formula fashion and formula consumer experiences may be 'easy' to manufacture for brands and retailers, but their effect is to mollify consumers and limit expectations. Formula fashion stifles the growth of alternatives, pushing down prices and making it uneconomic for small makers to compete in the market. The result is to further diminish choice. As a chain store replaces an independent store, distinctive products embodying local difference, flavour and fit are erased in the pursuit of standardized easy- and cheap-to-manufacture uniformity. While mass-manufacturing and cheap high street stores have provided us with more products to choose from, these choices are more restricted (ask anyone who is different to the 'standard' body shape about the difficulty of finding clothes to fit). The products on sale in our high streets are becoming homogeneous and this lack of choice erodes our individuality and dulls our imagination, limiting our confidence about what clothes can be.

Not only does the homogeneity of fashion on offer in the high street
have a pacifying effect on us as consumers, suppressing our expectations
and stifling our questions, but the products themselves are presented to us
as complete or 'closed', with an almost untouchable or sacrosanct status.
This dissuades us from personalizing them in order to make them our own.
It makes us wary of cutting off a collar, ripping out a lining or tucking a
waistband. Closed products are one-way information flows from designer
to consumer. Users 'follow' the trends prescribed by the industry elite and
become increasingly distanced from the creative practices surrounding
their clothes. This severing of the tie between users and skills marks a conspicuous cultural shift. As recently as two generations ago and for centuries
before that, textiles and garments were regularly made and maintained
by those who wore and used them, yet few people have those same skills
today. Ready-made garments appear to offer us the promise of something
better than we could make ourselves. Although when we go down the
route of buying into this perceived perfection, we end up forgoing an opportunity to learn how to make things and become better skilled.[2]

As deskilled individuals, we play into the hands of consumerist fashion. The fact that consumers can't do-it-themselves reinforces the fashion
system's current power structures and boosts the status of those at the top
because it resists input from outside. Further, the industry controls and
'professionalizes' the practice of designing and making clothes, resulting
in consumers having little idea how, from what and by whom these goods
are made. Instead a myth is created of a 'genius' designer, who synthesizes
trends, concepts and fabric into an inviolable piece. The result is deskilled
and ever more inactive individuals, who feel both unrepresented by the
fashion system and unable to do anything about it. The system, and the
clothes that represent it, appears to undermine our self-esteem and yet we
lack the knowledge and confidence to make, adapt and personalize fashion
pieces ourselves. From this position of passivity the only choice available to
us seems to be to consume.

New model of action

Participatory design offers an opportunity to change the power structures
associated with fashion and to produce garments by different means. This
could be as a result of a 'long conversation' between designers and users
or by individuals cutting, sewing and making garments themselves. These
approaches are implicit in a shift from quantity to quality that is central
to sustainability. This shift underpins many of the ideas explored in this

book, such as the move from wants to needs (Chapter 5), from global to lo-cal (Chapter 6), from fast to slow (Chapter 7), and now in this chapter, from consuming to making. This quality-based agenda promotes a new model of action that recognizes the importance of fashion to our culture but disassoci-ates it from the passivity, indifference and disengagement that is frequently induced by mass-market consumerist fashion. It is also concerned with the process of designing and making as a route to satisfying fundamental human needs – a significant step towards a deeper, more involved human culture.

These ideas are not new. In the 1970s, the cultural critic Ivan Illich wrote:

> I believe that a desirable future depends on our deliberately choosing a life of action, over a life of consumption. Rather than maintaining a lifestyle which only allows to produce and consume – a style of life which is merely a way station on the road to the depletion and pollution of the environment – the future depends upon our choice of institutions which support a life of action.[3]

Illich's ideas of a 'life of action' have major and multiple implications for sustainability and the relationships people have with their fashion and textiles today. People are recast in roles other than simply that of consumers; they are also competent individuals who are potential producers of their clothes, or suppliers of skills and resources enabling them to create as well as consume.

The idea of a life of action or the 'prosumer' (a portmanteau of producer and consumer) developed by Alvin Toffler,[4] again in the 1970s, challenges the consumer society's division of the world into either companies/manufacturers or consumers. The effect of this simplistic and market-driven partition is to relegate the practice of making clothes to the fringes of fashion activity and to the pages of specialist craft magazines and haberdashery stores, far away from glossy fashion titles and high street brands. There are, however, small signs of change. Quick to pick up on emerging trends, UK high street retailer TopShop recently offered one-off free craft workshops in some of its stores. And cool, feminist magazines like *Bust*[5] regularly run features on reworking clothes. *Bust* has also been at the forefront of a revival of interest in hand-knitting through its book *Stitch 'n Bitch*.[6]

Demos, a UK think-tank, has coined the term Pro-Am[7] (Professional Amateur) to describe this group of creative activists, who it sees as having an increasingly important role in our society and economy. These enthusias-tic amateurs, pursuing activities to professional standards, have substantial knowledge and skills that have been developed through experience and

▶ Hand-stitched recycled quilt by Alabama Chanin

over time. Demos calls this 'cultural capital', suggesting that this knowledge (which can't be bought) can improve our satisfaction with material consumption because when we are more confident about an activity we gain more pleasure from it. One study that looked at our favourite clothes seems to confirm this. It found that when people list their favourite clothes, handmade items were highly represented. It is suggested that having some control over our garments, either in a practical way through making, or more conceptually through influencing the design, brings people pleasure.[8]

Pro-Ams are thought to benefit in other ways from being active and creative. They have an improved sense of belonging, which flows from being part of a community where they collaborate, share ideas, learn from and teach each other; and a strong sense of self-worth, which makes them more resilient as people. These dedicated amateurs also play an important role in innovation, particularly in emerging fields (like say, sustainable fashion and textiles) that are too marginal to attract the interest of companies. They can, for example, pursue new ideas even when it appears there is no money to be made from them – and so aren't of interest to industry. Yet developing these ideas can eventually influence the way in which an industry operates, or test out how new, more sustainable products will actually be used in practice.

Pro-Am networks seem to offer the potential of a complementary mode of production for fashion that could facilitate a sustainability agenda based on local production. It could suit the needs of today's fashion designers as well as their global markets and at the same time use the considerable skills of individuals. This is a mode of production employed to great effect by Alabama Chanin in the making of its exquisite hand-stitched products.[9] These products enlist the craftsmanship of local artisans and strive to bring a contemporary context to age-old techniques.

Open-source design

One of the best examples of Pro-Am-led innovation is the Linux open-source software movement that was developed and continues to be driven by its unpaid and widely distributed user communities. Open-source initiatives, many of which are made possible by the Web, including blogs, Wikipedia and YouTube, are all built on the premise that people have skills and are willing to share them and can successfully collaborate on large-scale projects without being controlled by markets or management. In effect these initiatives put a stop to the one-way-only stream of information that flows from companies to consumers, and instead opens up new channels of messaging, material (re)use and innovation. They are seen by some sustainable designers as at the heart of a revitalization of design in a more ethical age;[10] and by others as a new type of democracy relevant to fashion, 'We should not only receive but also broadcast, not only consume, but also produce. Every reader is a potential writer and the language shall not be controlled by the provider. Free speech has to be fought for even in the fashion system.'[11]

Open source offers a more inclusive, ecological and engaging model for fashion and textiles. In open source people are active and progress towards a collective goal. They share the work and share the benefits. A sense of network is also important – while they may be autonomous individuals, they are also part of a bigger project. The key questions for us in fashion and textiles are: What is our shared goal? And what will it take to make it happen? From a sustainability perspective, any goal would have to include a mandate to transform underlying sustainability problems, including our addiction to consumption. One way to enact this is to shift from 'blind consumption' to 'reflective competence'[12] by developing expertise and knowledge about design and production. As suggested above, when we are actively engaged in, learning about or teaching something, we tend to feel more fulfilled. We are drawn out of a passive state where our focus and goal tends to be 'having' a garment and into the more active states of being (engaged and creative), doing (sewing) and interacting (with fashion symbolism). These active states have a requirement for an evolving set of knowledge and skills so that we don't become bored or frustrated. The aim is to enable us to engage in a process of enrichment that is chiefly concerned with skills, knowledge and experience and one where our focus is switched away from the accumulation of possessions to one where possessions, while still important, are used as tools to help us to become better skilled.

Importantly, open-source fashion isn't led or monopolized by megabrands or retailers – it takes fashion beyond the world of commerce; instead it is led by widely distributed individuals – consumers, creators and designers. This is in contrast with some eco-efficiency-led approaches to sustainable design, which are regularly led by large corporations (see Chapter 2). Instead it is an approach that flows from the small actions of creative individuals or communities and is characterized by being unscripted and improvisational. James Gustave Speth[13] has described these activities as 'green jazz' and sees them as a key way to promote sustainability:

> Jazz describes a world in which people harness situations and opportunities to find solutions and in the process create 'a complex market-led world of ad hoc experimentation'. It involves partnerships, alliances and fluidity to meet civil demands.[14]

Fashion and music have always influenced each other, and green jazz presents a new opportunity to do this in a sustainability context. It would involve exploring new ground and improvising and experimenting in different ways with new groups in order to develop products and projects for the common good.

More than a trend

In the last few years, user engagement has become a noticeable design trend, part of the 'supermarket of styles' promoted by post-modern design. Examples take the form of everything from underwear that is sold with fabric pens, to pieces like the Muji Freecut raincoat,[15] where the user is encouraged to cut along pre-printed lines on the sleeves, body and hood of the unisize coat to improve fit. While these products do have a different relationship with users, their raison d'être is rarely to challenge the top–down hierarchy of fashion. Participatory design is about a shift in emphasis away from control. It is part of a different world-view, where power distributions are changed, where there is greater transparency of the design and production process and where ideas about design, work and production are altered. Here we are interested in the transformative act of change that furnishes us with skills, products, relationships and experiences that allow us become better engaged with ourselves, each other and the material world.

Participatory design and designers

Participatory design is built on the idea that those who ultimately use a product are entitled to have a voice in determining how it is designed and that the quality of design increases if the stakeholders are included in the design process. The implication here is that everyone is a designer and that design is no longer just the work of specialists. Instead users (acting as designers) and designers themselves learn and create together. Designers still play a strategic role in the process, acting as a catalyst for product development, but they no longer exclusively control form, function or use.[16] This is a substantial change for many designers, as user involvement with the design process or extended user-engagement with the product is rarely part of the brief. If it happens at all, it tends to be something that happens in spite of the will of the designer, rather than because of it. When design is no longer about surface styling and more about promoting action, its aim is to increase the potential of the user and its focus becomes social change. The wearer is no longer a passive audience, but rather a co-creator and partner.

Otto von Busch describes this new role for designers as, 'a street level collaborative practical facilitator and creative teaser'.[17] The role of the creative teaser is to orchestrate change by creating the opportunities for people to work collaboratively. This role is more complex than the traditional design role and involves intense negotiation, steering a course between open conversations between stakeholders and the need to take practical action. It is also unpredictable, something that is an implicit part of working with cooperative processes. The garments or products produced may also look very different to those designed today. It is likely that they won't conform to visual norms, perhaps be 'clunky' and confusing (although they may of course be nicer too). As such these items may be rejected by mainstream fashion as unworkable or unattractive – but this misses the point. The products are concerned with the empowering act of user involvement and are a complement to, not a replacement for, other types of design production.

Suzy Gablik describes participatively designed products as rooted in a more ecologically and socially aware partnership model of aesthetics, which she sees as contrasting sharply with the dominator model of aesthetics that controls the visual agenda of art and design today. The dominator model is derived from a view where power is associated with

> ...authority, mastery, invulnerability and a strong association of ego-boundaries... By contrast in the partnership model, relationships are central and nothing stands alone in its own power or exists in isolation, independent of the larger framework or process in which it exists.[18]

The relationship model can already be seen as supporting a more participative process in other sectors. John Thackara,[19] for example, describes a new approach to medical care where the doctor and patient form a therapeutic alliance to promote health and prevent illness rather than acting as independent individuals only coming together when one needs the advice and medicine of the other. Participatory design in fashion and textiles is concerned with a similar therapeutic alliance between designer and user and attempts to empower individuals to become more engaged with the design and production of their products.

To make user involvement possible, the design and production process itself has to be made more transparent. This would aid a greater understanding of materials and of the culture they represent, so that we act not only on a practical, physical level, cutting and sewing fibres and garments, but also politically, ecologically and even economically. A more transparent process has, for example, allowed the Linux programmers to become a key economic and political force in the world of computer operating systems, so much so that Linux is now one of the biggest challengers to Microsoft. The same can be said for websites, like MySpace and YouTube, that have bypassed the traditional routes of music, film and video production by providing an opportunity to self-publish creative work, so challenging the dominance of traditional forms of broadcast media like television and radio. In the world of fashion, websites like Citizen Fashion,[20] an Internet gallery of clothing, showcases individuals' design creativity and making skills. Its aim it to put fashion in the hands of the people and in the process wrest back some of the power over what we wear from buyers, brands and retailers. The site is seen as a platform to share new ideas and collaborate on developing new styles. It is described as a small step towards democratizing fashion, where 'people all over the world become more empowered to share their view of fashion and help produce it for other people to enjoy'.

Participatory design reconnects maker and user, commonly by reframing the user as maker. To make user involvement practical for people it must be low tech and inexpensive.[21] This provides no barrier in fashion and textiles as most user involvement necessitates hand work with needle, thread and scissors or, at the most high tech, a domestic sewing machine. While the goal of participatory design is to devolve the role of the creator and promote action and participation in users, a key spin-off of many of these design processes is that they can in a small, widely dispersed way lead to a reduction in what we buy and discard. They do this by infusing a product with the user's touch, giving it a different and hopefully richer product meaning that means that it will be worn and found pleasurable, for longer.

The remainder of this chapter is dedicated to a small selection of examples of participatory design in fashion and textiles. In some of these examples, their aim is to devolve the role of creator. For others, user-engagement is used as a route to producing more customized and unique products. For others still, user interaction is designed-in as the only way to produce a fully functioning and complete item. The ground between fashion and textiles and participatory design processes (that is, fabrics and garments designed and made *with* rather than *for* people) is little explored and potentially abundant, perhaps because it is complex ground in which to affect change. Yet with each new wave of interest in sustainability comes a deeper understanding of the issues associated with fashion and textiles – making it likely that participatory design and individual and social action will probably define an important component of sustainable fashion and textiles activity into the future.

Reform

In the Reform project,[22] the fashion designer, activist and researcher, Otto von Busch, freely distributes a series of DIY methods for remaking new pieces from old garments. He describes them as 'cook books' and produces collections of methods (not collections of garments) where the aim is to teach basic skills to liberate the 'chef' from the buying of ready-made pre-packaged items (which is the category in which von Busch places most high street fashion in today). Reform's aim is to elevate cutting, sewing and making into micro-political acts that subvert current power structures in the fashion sector and are, 'an insurrection against a state of (consumer) resignation'.[23] These acts are seen as a way for users to intrude into the closed world of fashion production, but still tap into the global fashion system and use its magical

▼ High bag pants by Wronsov a.k.a. Otto von Busch

Short sleeve
suit, vest suit
and oblique
collar shirt by
Wronsov a.k.a.
Otto von
Busch

and culturally rich symbolism as a tool for wider expression and participation. von Busch is clear that the act of reform is political in nature and describes the reforming of clothes as a way to reprogramme these garments' meaning when their fashionable image has gone 'dry' and then insert them back into the fashion system, 'acting in reverse consumerism'.

The Reform methods form part of von Busch's extensive work in this area, the effects of which he sees in broad terms:

> They reawaken a spirit by lowering the threshold to own activity and give immediate response in social situations. They give voice to the silent by breaking the pacifying system of consumption. They build self-reliance by teaching basic skills and improving an understanding of reform. They mobilize resources by using recycled material often with personal connection. They make micro plans by creating other forms of social organisation.[24]

In his most recent collection of methods (autumn/winter 2007), von Busch details eight different reform techniques for menswear including the re-styling of shirts, trousers and jackets. For each method a photographic step-by-step process is provided, as is a list of items needed to make the transformation.

Matrushka

Matrushka[25] is both a retail space and production unit run by two designers in Los Angeles. It was set up to provide an alternative to more conventional ways of garment production and shopping. The company's ethos and its clothing lines are based on political and environmental awareness and on taking action. Matrushka's motto is 'fashion for the people' and what is produced is a combination of collaborative design, personalized fit and hands-on tailoring. Several times a year, Matrushka runs T-construction nights where the customer is brought together with a special assembly line for a night of local fashion activism and 'raucous creation'. The customer selects and orders a customized T-shirt from a 'menu' of pre-printed patches, sizes and colours and then follows the making of the garment from beginning to end; watching as local designers, artists and seamstresses sew the parts together. The event is part recreation, where drinks and DJs are mixed with the pattern pieces, and part creation, where the customer becomes part of the design process.

Do shirt

The do shirt[26] is one of a range of products developed in collaboration between do and Droog design, called dosurf. The collaboration's aim was to promote a more dissipated approach to production that encourages users to shape their own products. The do shirt was designed expressly for user interaction; the T-shirt can't be worn until the owner has played their part. The do shirt is huge – ten times too big – but the claim is that this makes it ten times more useful. The T-shirt comes with a booklet of do shirt sculptures plus an invitation to contribute to the do shirt exhibition. The product only comes alive when the user adds his/her own interpretation, and because it is hard to wear the T-shirt in the same way twice, each time the garment is worn it is in effect an unique piece and far beyond the control of the designer.

▲ T-construction night at Matrushka

▶ do shirt by do/ KesselsKramer

Updatable

Fashion clothes capture a moment in time and are as quickly forgotten. But what if that moment was not one but many moments, a process of transformation? What if that process required you to reach into the sewing kit and update that garment yourself? The Updatable T-shirt was developed as part of the 5 Ways research project[27] and involved users making a series of transformations to a T-shirt. Updatable was concerned about a switch in emphasis: from one garment to many garments; from passive consumers to active users; from a single snapshot in time to an ongoing movie. This project's aim was to build skills and confidence and to promote a greater understanding of the many small processes at work in creating a garment and encourage people to 'do-it-yourself'. Layered on top of this capability-inducing agenda was a desire to reduce material consumption by cutting, stitching and styling a piece. The project involved design ideas; methods and props being sent through the post to a small group of users, who then interpreted the instructions and produced a singularly stylish piece that they documented and wore over the next months. What resulted was a widely eclectic range of garments that emerged out of a unique collaboration based on change.

▼ Updatable T-shirt produced as part of the 5 Ways Project

Notes

Introduction

1   Ehrenfeld, J. R. (2004), Searching for sustainability: No quick fix, *Reflections*, 5(8), p10.

2   Pepper, D. (1996), *Modern Environmentalism: An Introduction*, London: Routledge, p37.

3   Simon, H. as quoted by Thackara, J. (2005), *In the Bubble*, Boston: MIT Press, p1.

Chapter 1

1   Simpson, P. (2006), Global trends in fibre prices, production and consumption, *Textiles Outlook International*, 125, pp82–106.

2   Simpson, P. (2006), Global trends in fibre prices, production and consumption, *Textiles Outlook International*, 125, pp82–106.

3   Simpson, P. (2006), Global trends in fibre prices, production and consumption, *Textiles Outlook International*, 125, pp82–106.

4   Laursen, S. E. and Hansen, J. (1997), *Environmental Assessment of Textiles*, Copenhagen: Danish Environmental Protection Agency, p46.

5   Myers, D. (1999), Organic cotton: A more sustainable approach, in D. Myers and S. Stolton (eds), *Organic Cotton: From Field to Final Product*, London: Intermediate Technology Publications, p8.

6   Laursen, S. E. and Hansen, J. (1997), *Environmental Assessment of Textiles*, Copenhagen: Danish Environmental Protection Agency, pp31–51; Myers, D. (1999), The problems with conventional cotton, in D. Myers and S. Stolton (eds), *Organic Cotton: From Field to Final Product*, London, Intermediate Technology Publications, pp8–20.

7   Myers, D. (1999), Organic cotton: A more sustainable approach, in D. Myers and S. Stolton (eds), *Organic Cotton: From Field to Final Product*, London, Intermediate Technology Publications, p11.

8   Allwood, J. M., Laursen, S. E., Malvido de Rodriguez, C. and Bocken, N. M. P. (2006), *Well Dressed?*, Cambridge: University of Cambridge Institute of Manufacturing, p45.

9   Laursen, S. E. and Hansen, J. (1997), *Environmental Assessment of Textiles*, Copenhagen: Danish Environmental Protection Agency, p51.

10 Cupit, M. J. (1996), *Opportunities and Barriers to Textile Recycling*, Abingdon, Oxfordshire: AEA Technology, p14.

11 *ENDS Report* (2006), Directorate suspends cypermethrin sheep dips, No. 374, p15.

12 European Commission (2003), Integrated Pollution Prevention and Control Reference Document on Best Available Techniques for the Textiles Industry, Brussels: European Commission, p30.

13 UNEP (1993), *The Textile Industry and the Environment*, Industry and the Environment Technical Report No. 16, Paris: United Nations Publications, p22.

14 Slater, K. (2003), *Environmental Impact of Textiles: Production, Processes and Protection*, Cambridge: Woodhead Publishing, p27.

15 Kozlowski, R., Mankowski, J. and Baraniecki, P. (1994), Bast fibre crops cultivated on polluted soils, in The Textile Institute, *World Conference Proceedings 1994*, Manchester: The Textile Institute, pp167–174.

16 Riddlestone, S., Desai, P., Evans, M. and Skyring, A. (1994), *Bioregional

Fibres: The Potential for a Sustainable Regional Paper and Textile Industry Based on Flax and Hemp, Surrey: Bioregional Development Group, pp50–56.

17   Laursen, S. E. and Hansen, J. (1997), *Environmental Assessment of Textiles*, Copenhagen: Danish Environmental Protection Agency, p84.

18   Laursen, S. E. and Hansen, J. (1997), *Environmental Assessment of Textiles*, Copenhagen: Danish Environmental Protection Agency, p85.

19   See for example EU Eco-labelling Board (1997), *Establishment of Ecological Criteria for Textile Products*, Second Interim Report, B4-3040/96/00470/MAR/E4.

20   Allwood, J. M., Laursen, S. E., Malvido de Rodriguez, C. and Bocken, N. M. P. (2006), *Well Dressed?*, Cambridge: University of Cambridge Institute of Manufacturing, p29.

21   *ENDS Report* (1996), Du Pont outlines plans to curb nylon N2O emissions, No. 260, pp7–8.

22   Laursen, S. E. and Hansen, J. (1997), *Environmental Assessment of Textiles*, Copenhagen: Danish Environmental Protection Agency, p101.

23   Laursen, S. E. and Hansen, J. (1997), *Environmental Assessment of Textiles*, Copenhagen: Danish Environmental Protection Agency, pp69–79.

24   Swaminathan, K. and Manonmani, K. (1997), Studies on toxicity of viscose rayon factory effluents. Part 1: Effect on water, *Journal of Environmental Biology*, 18(1), pp73–78.

25   *ENDS Report* (1994), The elusive consensus on lifecycle assessment, No. 231, pp20–22.

26   DuPont Environmental Excellence Team (undated), *Man Made Fibres and the Environment*, Gloucester: DuPont.

27   Raninger, F. (1996), Cellulosics and environmental protection, *Textile Asia*, September, pp62–64, 73.

28   Schmidtbauer, J. (1996), Clean production of rayon – an eco-inventory, in proceedings of Conference *Imagine the Future of Viscose Technology*, Gmunden, Austria.

29   Laursen, S. E. and Hansen, J. (1997), *Environmental Assessment of Textiles*, Copenhagen: Danish Environmental Protection Agency.

30   Laursen, S. E. and Hansen, J. (1997), *Environmental Assessment of Textiles*, Copenhagen: Danish Environmental Protection Agency, p46.

31   Laursen, S. E. and Hansen, J. (1997), *Environmental Assessment of Textiles*, Copenhagen: Danish Environmental Protection Agency.

32   Drury, K. and Slater, K. (1996), Fibres and the environment, *Textile Trends*, June, pp29–33.

33   Walsh, J. A. H. and Brown, M. S. (1995), Pricing environmental impacts: A tale of two T-shirts, *Illahee*, 11(3–4), pp175–182.

34   Walsh, J. A. H. and Brown, M. S. (1995), Pricing environmental impacts: a tale of two T-shirts, *Illahee*, 11(3–4), p177.

35   Franklin Associates (1993), Resource and Environmental Profile Analysis of a Manufactured Apparel Product: Woman's knit polyester blouse, Washington DC: American Fiber Manufacturers Association.

36   Allwood, J. M., Laursen, S. E., Malvido de Rodriguez, C. and Bocken, N. M. P. (2006), *Well Dressed?*, Cambridge: University of Cambridge Institute of Manufacturing.

37   van Elzakker, B. (1999), Organic cotton production, in D. Myers and S. Stolton (eds), *Organic Cotton: From Field to Final Product*, London: Intermediate Technology Publications, p22.

38   Allwood, J. M., Laursen, S. E., Malvido de Rodriguez, C. and Bocken, N. M. P. (2006), *Well Dressed?*, Cambridge: University of Cambridge Institute of Manufacturing, p47.

39   Allwood, J. M., Laursen, S. E., Malvido de Rodriguez, C. and Bocken, N. M. P. (2006), *Well Dressed?*, Cambridge: University of Cambridge Institute of Manufacturing, p47.

40   Soil Association (2007), *Organic Standards*, Bristol: Soil Association, Chapter 60.

41   www.soilassociation.org/

42   www.sustainablecotton.org

43   Grose, L. (2007), Back to basics, *EcoTextile News*, No. 4, pp24–25.

44   International Cotton Advisory Committee (2004), Report of the second expert panel on biotechnology of cotton, Washington DC: International Cotton Advisory Committee, p2.

45   International Cotton Advisory Committee (2004), Report of the second expert panel on biotechnology of cotton, Washington DC: International Cotton Advisory Committee, p5.

46   International Cotton Advisory Committee (2004), Report of the second expert panel on biotechnology of cotton, Washington DC: International Cotton Advisory Committee, p32.

47   *ENDS Report* (2003), GM crops have 'increased pesticide use', No. 347, pp13–14.

48   www.bettercotton.org/

49   Heming, Z. (2007), Esquel steps in the right direction, *EcoTextile News*, No. 3, p14–15.

50   www.fairtrade.org.uk/products_cotton.htm

51   PAN UK (2007), *My Sustainable T-shirt*, London: PAN UK, p20.

52   www.illuminati2-noir.com/

53   www.unglobalcompact.org/

54   www.isleofmullweavers.com/

55   Alden, D. M, Proops, J. L. R. and Gay, P. W. (1996), *Industrial Hemp's Double Dividend: A Study for the USA*, The University of Melbourne, Department of Economics, Research Paper 528.

56   Mohan Rao, K. (2007), Tasar culture and forest policy – constraints and guidelines, *Indian Silk,* 145(10), pp14–18.

57   Slater, K. (2003), *Environmental Impact of Textiles: Production, Processes and Protection*, Cambridge: Woodhead Publishing, p27.

58   *EcoTextile News* (2007), PLA composting project recognised, No. 3, p9.

59   *ENDS Report* (2003), DuPont joins race to offer biopolymers, No. 346, pp32–33.

60   Blackburn, R. S. (2005), Introduction, in R. S. Blackburn (ed), *Biodegradable and Sustainable Fibres*, Cambridge: Woodhead Publishing, pxvii.

61   Hemmings, J. (2007), Corn on the job, *EcoTextile News*, No. 2, pp16–17.

62   Vink et al, as cited by Farrington, D. W., Lunt, J., Davies, S. and Blackburn, R. S. (2005), Poly(lactic acid) fibres, in R. S. Blackburn (ed), *Biodegradable and Sustainable Fibres*, Cambridge: Woodhead Publishing, pp212–215.

63   White, P., Hyhurst, M., Taylor, J. and Slater, A. (2005), Lyocell fibres, in R. S. Blackburn (ed), *Biodegradable and Sustainable Fibres*, Cambridge: Woodhead Publishing, pp157–190.

64   White, P., Hyhurst, M., Taylor, J. and Slater, A. (2005), Lyocell fibres, in R. S. Blackburn (ed), *Biodegradable and Sustainable Fibres*, Cambridge: Woodhead Publishing, pp171.

65   www.bamboo-t-shirt.com/

66   Brooks, M. M. (2005), Soya bean protein fibres – past, present and future, in R. S. Blackburn (ed), *Biodegradable and Sustainable Fibres*, Cambridge: Woodhead Publishing, pp398–440.

67   Rainsford, F. (2007), Cotton with altitude, *EcoTextile News*, No. 1, p22.

68   www.perunaturtex.com/

69   Department of the Environment (1993), *A Novel Use for Recycled Textile Fibres*, Good practice case study No. 181, London: DoE.

70   www.anniesherburne.co.uk

71   www.unifi-inc.com/

72   www.polartec.com/

Chapter 2

1   See for example *ENDS Report* (2007), Textile firm fined for pollution and IPPC failures, No. 385, p10; *ENDS Report* (2002), Rochdale dyeing

firm fined for bleach pollution, No. 328, p58; *ENDS Report* (2000), Textiles business fined under council's nuisance powers, No. 304, p55.

2   *ENDS Report* (2004), IPPC makes 'poorly managed' textile firms pull their socks up, No. 356, pp8–9.

3   Fashioning an Ethical Industry (undated), *Working conditions in the global fashion industry*, Factsheet 6, www.fashioninganethicalindustry. org, p1.

4   *ENDS Report* (2006), Retailers to train suppliers on chemical risks, No. 273, p23.

5   *ENDS Report* (2004), Tests mandated for azo dyes, No. 359, p55.

6   European Commission (2003), Integrated Pollution Prevention and Control Reference Document on Best Available Techniques for the Textiles Industry, Brussels: European Commission.

7   http://ec.europa.eu/environment/chemicals/reach/reach_intro.htm

8   www.csr.gov.uk/whatiscsr.shtml

9   www.corporate-responsibility.org/C2B/PressOffice/display. asp?ID=74&Type=2

10   www.fuk.co.uk/blog/marian/ethical_evolution_topshop

11   The No Logo debate was initiated by Naomi Klein's book of the same name: Klein, N. (2000), *No Logo*, London: HarperCollins.

12   European Commission (2003), Integrated Pollution Prevention and Control Reference Document on Best Available Techniques for the Textiles Industry, Brussels: European Commission, ppii–iii.

13   UNEP (1993), *The Textile Industry and the Environment*, Industry and the Environment Technical Report No. 16, Paris: United Nations Publications, p48.

14   European Commission (2003), Integrated Pollution Prevention and Control Reference Document on Best Available Techniques for the Textiles Industry, Brussels: European Commission, p450.

15   European Commission (2003), Integrated Pollution Prevention and Control Reference Document on Best Available Techniques for the Textiles Industry, Brussels: European Commission, p288.

16   Allwood, J. M., Laursen, S. E., Malvido de Rodriguez, C. and Bocken, N. M. P. (2006), *Well Dressed?*, Cambridge: University of Cambridge Institute of Manufacturing, p33.

17   *Textile Horizons* (2003), The future of knitting available today, November–December, pp21–22.

18   UNEP (1993), *The Textile Industry and the Environment*, Industry and the Environment Technical Report No. 16, Paris: United Nations Publications, p38.

19   Soil Association (2007), *Soil Association Organic Standards*, Bristol: Soil Association, Chapter 60 – Textiles.

20   www.climatex.com

21   European Commission (2003), Integrated Pollution Prevention and Control Reference Document on Best Available Techniques for the Textiles Industry, Brussels: European Commission, pp293–296.

22   Laursen, S. E. and Hansen, J. (1997), *Environmental Assessment of Textiles*, Copenhagen: Danish Environmental Protection Agency, p124.

23   UNEP (1993), *The Textile Industry and the Environment*, Industry and the Environment Technical Report No. 16, Paris: United Nations Publications, p40.

24   Cooper, P. (1992), The consequences of new environmental legislation on the UK textile industry, *Textiles Horizons International*, 12(10), pp30–38.

25   European Commission (2003), Integrated Pollution Prevention and Control Reference Document on Best Available Techniques for the Textiles Industry, Brussels: European Commission, pp304–357.

26   UNEP (1993), *The Textile Industry and the Environment*, Industry and the Environment Technical Report No. 16, Paris: United Nations Publications, pp54–55.

27   Milmo, S. (2007), Developments in textile colorants, *Textile Outlook International*, January–February, p28.

28   Milmo, S. (2007), Developments in textile colorants, *Textile Outlook International*, January–February, pp26–28.

29   Lewis, D. M. (1997), Colouration 2000, *Journal of Society of Dyers and Colourists*, 113, July/August, p196.

30   www.biomatnet.org/secure/Air/F223.htm

31   European Commission (2003), Integrated Pollution Prevention and Control Reference Document on Best Available Techniques for the Textiles Industry, Brussels: European Commission, pp451–453.

32   Milmo, S. (2007), Developments in textile colorants, *Textile Outlook International*, January–February, p38.

33   UNEP (1993), *The Textile Industry and the Environment*, Industry and the Environment Technical Report No. 16, Paris: United Nations Publications, p56.

34   European Commission (2003), Integrated Pollution Prevention and Control Reference Document on Best Available Techniques for the Textiles Industry, Brussels: European Commission, pp453–454.

35   *ENDS Report* (2004), Perfluorinated chemicals: Jumping from frying pan into fire?, No. 354, pp28–31.

36   *ENDS Report* (2007), Tackling a grubby reputation, No. 386, pp30–33.

37   European Commission (2003), Integrated Pollution Prevention and Control Reference Document on Best Available Techniques for the Textiles Industry, Brussels: European Commission, pp373–393.

38   Fashioning an Ethical Industry (undated), *The structure of the fashion industry*, Factsheet 2, www.fashioninganethicalindustry.org.

39   Fashioning an Ethical Industry (undated), *Life after the MFA*, Factsheet 4, www.fashioninganethicalindustry.org.

40   War on Want (2006), *Fashion Victims: The True Cost of Cheap Clothes at Primark, Asda and Tesco*, www.waronwant.org/Fashion+Victims+13593.twl

41   www.oxfam.org/en/policy/briefingnotes/offside_labor_report

42   www.cleanclothes.org/ftp/06-09-cleanupfashion.pdf

43   www.cleanclothes.org/codes/ccccode.htm

44   www.sa-intl.org/

45   Fashioning an Ethical Industry (undated), *A brief history of company engagement*, Factsheet 9, www.fashioninganethicalindustry.org

46   www.ethicaltrade.org/

47   Meadows, D. H. (1997), Places to intervene in a system, *Whole Earth*, Winter, www.wholeearthmag.com/ArticleBin/109.html

48   www.marksandspencer.com/

49   Fashioning an Ethical Industry (undated), *The fashion industry and poverty reduction*, Factsheet 3a, www.fashioninganethicalindustry.org, p3.

50   Allwood, J. M., Laursen, S. E., Malvido de Rodriguez, C. and Bocken, N. M. P. (2006), *Well Dressed?* Cambridge: University of Cambridge Institute of Manufacturing, p12.

51   www.edun.ie/one.asp

52   www.aidtoartisans.org/

53   www.made-by.nl

54   www.peopletree.co.uk/

55   www.americanapparel.net/

56   www.dosainc.com/

57   Meadows, D. H. (1997), Places to intervene in a system, *Whole Earth*, Winter, www.wholeearthmag.com/ArticleBin/109.html

Chapter 3

1   Uitdenbogerd, D. E., Brouwer, N. M. and Groot-Marcus, J. P. (1998), *Domestic Energy Saving Potentials for Food and Textiles: An Empirical Study*. Wageningen, NL: Wageningen Agricultural University.

2   Franklin Associates (1993), Resource and Environmental Profile Analysis of a Manufactured Apparel Product: Woman's knit polyester blouse, Washington DC: American Fiber Manufacturers Association, pp3–4.

3   Allwood, J. M., Laursen, S. E., Malvido de Rodriguez, C. and Bocken,

N. M. P. (2006), *Well Dressed?*, Cambridge: University of Cambridge Institute of Manufacturing, p43.

4   Allwood, J. M., Laursen, S. E., Malvido de Rodriguez, C. and Bocken, N. M. P. (2006), *Well Dressed?*, Cambridge: University of Cambridge Institute of Manufacturing, p29.

5   Franklin Associates (1993), Resource and Environmental Profile Analysis of a Manufactured Apparel Product: Woman's knit polyester blouse, Washington DC: American Fiber Manufacturers Association.

6   Table adapted from Paakkunainen, R. (1995), *Textiles and the Environment*, Eindhoven: European Design Centre.

7   Heiskanen, E. (2002), The institutional logic of life cycle thinking, *Journal of Cleaner Production*, 10, p429.

8   Franklin Associates (1993), Resource and Environmental Profile Analysis of a Manufactured Apparel Product: Woman's knit polyester blouse, Washington DC: American Fiber Manufacturers Association, ppES–8.

9   Franklin Associates (1993), Resource and Environmental Profile Analysis of a Manufactured Apparel Product: Woman's knit polyester blouse, Washington DC: American Fiber Manufacturers Association.

10   Franklin Associates (1993), Resource and Environmental Profile Analysis of a Manufactured Apparel Product: Woman's knit polyester blouse, Washington DC: American Fiber Manufacturers Association, pp3–4.

11   Allwood, J. M., Laursen, S. E., Malvido de Rodriguez, C. and Bocken, N. M. P. (2006), *Well Dressed?* Cambridge: University of Cambridge Institute of Manufacturing, p40.

12   Allwood, J. M., Laursen, S. E., Malvido de Rodriguez, C. and Bocken, N. M. P. (2006), *Well Dressed?* Cambridge: University of Cambridge Institute of Manufacturing, p47.

13   Brezet, H. (1997), Dynamics in ecodesign practice, *UNEP Industry and Environment*, January–June, pp21–24.

14   *ENDS Report* (2001), M&S recommends cooler clothes wash to save energy, No. 319, p32.

15   Allwood, J. M., Laursen, S. E., Malvido de Rodriguez, C. and Bocken, N. M. P. (2006), *Well Dressed?* Cambridge: University of Cambridge Institute of Manufacturing, p40.

16   *ENDS Report* (2007), Calls for energy labelling overhaul as sales of efficient white goods stall, No. 329, p32.

17   Fletcher, K. and Goggin, P. (2001), The dominant stances on ecodesign: A critique, *Design Issues*, 17(3), pp15–25.

18   *ENDS Report* (2002), Consumption cutbacks 'on track', say laundry detergent producers, No. 337, p33.

19   *ENDS Report* (2003), Surfactant producers claim that water consumption is the real issue, No. 337, p33.

20   *ENDS Report* (2001), Sanyo's zero-detergent washing machine, No. 319, p32.

21   Sawa, K., Rodriguez, C., Aramaki, K. and Kunieda, H. (2003), A new detergent-free dry-cleaning system, *International Journal of Clothing Science and Technology*, 16(30), pp324–334.

22   Robert van den Hoed (1997), Sustainable washing of clothes, *Towards Sustainable Product Design conference proceedings*, Farnham, UK: The Centre for Sustainable Design, unpaginated.

23   Aumônier, S. and Collins, M. (2005), *Life Cycle Assessment of Disposable and Reusable Nappies in the UK*, Bristol: Environment Agency.

24   www.marksandspencer.com/gp/node/n/50713031?ie=UTF8&mnSBran d=core

25   *ENDS Report* (2001), M&S recommends cooler clothes wash to save energy, No. 319, p32.

26   *ENDS Report* (2004), Perfluorinated chemicals: Jumping from frying pan into fire? No. 354, pp28–31.

27   Qin, Y. (2004), Silver streak, *Textile Horizons*, November–December, pp16–17.

28   *ENDS Report* (2007), Tackling a grubby reputation, No. 386, pp30–33.

29   *ENDS Report* (2003), Retailers step back from triclosan, No. 345, p35.

30   Blackburn, R. and Payne, J. (2004), Life cycle analysis of cotton towels: Impact of domestic laundering and recommendations for extending periods between washing, *Green Chemistry*, 6, G59–G61.

31   Catton, G. (2007), *Sustainable Cleaning, Fast, Affordable and Sustainable Fashion*, ASBCI Conference proceedings, 17 May 2007.

32   See for example Charter, M. and Tischner, U. (eds) (2001), *Sustainable Solutions: Developing Products and Services for the Future*, Sheffield: Greenleaf.

33   www.5ways.info

34   Thorpe, A. (2007), *The Designer's Atlas of Sustainability*, Washington DC: Island Press, p193.

35   *Textile Outlook International* (2006), Innovations in fibres, textiles, apparel and machinery, November–December, p90.

36   Tomes, N. (1997), Spreading the Germ Theory: Sanitary Science and Home Economics 1880–1930, in S. Stage and V. B. Vincenti (eds), *Rethinking Home Economics*, New York: Cornell Univesrity Press.

37   Hoy, S. (1995), *Chasing Dirt: The American Pursuit of Cleanliness*, New York: Oxford University Press, p171.

Chapter 4

1 The Fiftyrx3 blog, 'perusing the crossroads of style and sustainability' http://fiftyrx3.blogspot.com/

2 www.patagonia.com/

3 www.looolo.ca/index.html

4 Allwood, J. M., Laursen, S. E., Malvido de Rodriguez, C. and Bocken, N. M. P. (2006), *Well Dressed?*, Cambridge: University of Cambridge Institute of Manufacturing, p16.

5 Cupit, M. J. (1996), *Opportunities and Barriers to Textile Recycling*, Abingdon, Oxfordshire: AEA Technology, p21.

6 Allwood, J. M., Laursen, S. E., Malvido de Rodriguez, C. and Bocken, N. M. P. (2006), *Well Dressed?*, Cambridge: University of Cambridge Institute of Manufacturing, p12.

7 *ENDS Report* (2007), MEPs strengthen waste framework directive, No. 386, p53.

8 Jackson, T. (1996), *Material Concerns*, London: Routledge, p2.

9 Laursen, S. E., Alwood, J. M., De Brito, M. P. and Malvido De Rodriguez, C. (2005), *Sustainable Recovery of Products and Materials – Scenario Analysis of the UK Clothing and Textile Sector*, Design and Manufacture for Sustainable Development, 4th International Conference, Newcastle, 12–13 July.

10 Allwood, J. M., Laursen, S. E., Malvido de Rodriguez, C. and Bocken, N. M. P. (2006), *Well Dressed?*, Cambridge: University of Cambridge Institute of Manufacturing, p12.

11 See for example www.swapstyle.com/

12 See for example Linden Ivarsson, A-S., Brieditis, K. and Evans, K. (2005), *Second Time Cool: The Art of Chopping Up a Sweater*, Buffalo: Annick Press.

13 Traid Remade www.traid.org.uk/custom.html

14 Junky Styling www.junkystyling.co.uk/

15 www.anniesherburne.co.uk

16 www.mujionline.co.uk/catalogue/catalogue.asp?Sec=6&Sub=30&PID=262

17 www.unifi-inc.com/

18 www.polartec.com/

19 McDonough, W. and Braungart, M. (2002), *Cradle to Cradle*, New York: North Point Press, p58.

20 Recyclon recycled nylon by Toray Industries, Japan www.toray.com/

21 *EcoTextile News* (2007), Toray offers recycled nylon, No. 4, p23.

22   Keoleian, G. A. and Menerey, D. (1993), *Life Cycle Design Guidance Manual,* Washington DC: Environmental Protection Agency.

23   Cupit, M. J. (1996), *Opportunities and Barriers to Textile Recycling,* Abingdon, Oxfordshire: AEA Technology.

24   Laursen, S. E., Alwood, J. M., De Brito, M. P. and Malvido De Rodriguez, C. (2005), *Sustainable Recovery of Products and Materials – Scenario Analysis of the UK Clothing and Textile Sector,* Design and Manufacture for Sustainable Development, 4th International Conference, Newcastle, 12–13 July.

25   www.vaude.de

26   McDonough, W. and Braungart, M. (2002), *Cradle to Cradle,* New York: North Point Press, p62.

27   Holmgren, D. (2002), *Permaculture: Principles and Pathways Beyond Sustainability*, Victoria: Holmgren Design Services, p115.

28   Chapman, J. (2005), *Emotionally Durable Design: Objects, Experiences and Empathy*, London: Earthscan, p8.

29   Ehrenfeld, J. R. (2004), Searching for sustainability: No quick fix, *Reflections*, 5(8), p7.

30   www.o2.org/

31   www.5ways.info/

32   www.patagonia.com/pdf/en_US/common_thread_exec_summary.pdf

33   *ENDS Report* (2003), Making local connections for sustainability, No. 339, p29.

34   McDonough, W. and Braungart, M. (2002) *Cradle to Cradle*, New York: North Point Press.

35   www.climatex.com

36   www.trigema.de

37   www.victor-innovatex.com/

38   *ENDS Report* (2001), Council agrees on WEEE, No. 317, p37.

Chapter 5

1   Campbell, C. (2006), Consuming goods and the good of consuming, in T. Jackson (ed), *The Earthscan Reader in Sustainable Consumption*, London: Earthscan, p284.

2   Lee, M. (2003), *Fashion Victim: Our Love-Hate Relationship with Dressing, Shopping, and the Cost of Style*, New York: Broadway Books.

3   *Textile View* (1993), Trends, Issue 22, p17.

4   von Busch, O. (2005), *Re-forming Appearance: Subversive Strategies in the Fashion System – Reflections on Complementary Modes of Production*, Research Paper, www.selfpassage.org

5   Max-Neef, M. (1992), Development and human needs, in P. Ekins and M. Max-Neef (eds), *Real-life Economics*, London: Routledge, pp197–214.

6   These ideas are explored further by Thorpe, A. (2007), *The Designer's Atlas to Sustainability*, Washington DC: Island Press, p118.

7   Max-Neef, M. (1992), Development and human needs, in P. Ekins and M. Max-Neef (eds), *Real-life Economics*, London: Routledge, p202.

8   Ehrenfeld, J. R. (2004), Searching for sustainability: No quick fix, *Reflections*, 5(8), p7.

9   www.5ways.info/docs/projects/super/projects.htm

10   Manzini, E. (1994), Design, environment and social quality: From 'existenzminimum' to 'quality maximum', *Design Issues*, 10(1), pp37–43.

11   Berger, J. (1972), *Ways of Seeing*, London: Penguin Books.

12   www.bath.ac.uk/carpp/publications/coop_inquiry.html

13   Gablik, S. (1991), *The Re-enchantment of Art*, London: Thames and Hudson, p62.

14   Gablik, S. (1991), *The Re-enchantment of Art*, London: Thames and Hudson.

15   www.howies.co.uk

16   Shove, E. and Ward, A. (2002), Inconspicuous consumption, in R. E. Dunlap, F. H. Buttel, P. Dickens and A. Gijswijt (eds), *Sociological Theory and the Environment*, Boston USA: Rowman and Littlefield, pp230–251.

17   www.made-by.nl/

18   Randerson, J. (2007), Smart clothes to power your iPod or light your home … just don't wash them, *The Guardian*, 13 July, p3.

Chapter 6

1   Benyus, J. (1997), *Biomimicry*, New York: Quill Press.

2   www.speedo.com/

3   www.teijinfiber.com/sozai/sozain_emorpho.html

4   Benyus, J. (1997), *Biomimicry*, New York: Quill Press, p291.

5   This figure was mentioned in a recent Ecologist publication to coincide with London Fashion Week: Lee, M. and Sevier, L. (2007), *Sacking the Sackcloth Image: Ethical Fashion Special*, London: Ecologist, p13.

6   Walsh, J. A. H. and Brown, M. S. (1995), Pricing environmental impacts: A tale of two T-shirts, *Illahee*, 11(3–4), pp175–182.

7   Fashioning an Ethical Industry (undated), *The special challenge of China*, Factsheet 12a, www.fashioninganethicalindustry.org.

8   Benyus, J. (1997), *Biomimicry,* New York: Quill Press, p276.

9   Pepper, D. (1996), *Modern Environmentalism,* London: Routledge, p306.

10   Pepper, D. (1996), *Modern Environmentalism,* London: Routledge, p306.

11   McDonough, W. and Braungart, M. (2002) *Cradle to Cradle,* New York: North Point Press, p120.

12   Thackara, J. (2005), *In the Bubble,* Cambridge, Massachusetts: The MIT Press, p94.

13   Walker, S. (2006), *Sustainable by Design,* London: Earthscan, p128.

14   www.alabamachanin.com/

15   Manzini, E. and Jégou, F. (2003), *Sustainable Everyday: Scenarios for Urban Life,* Milan: Edizioni Ambiente.

16   Allwood, J. M., Laursen, S. E., Malvido de Rodriguez, C. and Bocken, N. M. P. (2006), *Well Dressed?,* Cambridge: University of Cambridge Institute of Manufacturing, p32.

17   www.adidas.com/campaigns/miadidas_teaser/content/?strcountry_adidascom=com

18   Tait, N. (2004), Mass customisation already a reality, *Textile Horizons,* January–February, pp13–17.

19   www.landsend.com/

20   www.sristi.org/honeybee.html

21   Taylor, J., Oram, J. and Kjell, P. (2004), *Clone Town Britain: The Survey,* London: New Economics Foundation, p28.

22   See for example Garthenor's organic woollen yarn made from rare breed sheep native to the UK, http://organicwoollies.co.uk/

23   www.bioregional.com/

24   www.ardalanishfarm.co.uk/

25   www.looolo.ca/

26   www.5ways.info/docs/projects/local/projects.htm

27   For more of an exploration of these ideas, see: Beukers, A. and van Hinte, E. (2005), *Lightness: The Inevitable Renaissance of Minimum Energy Structures,* Rotterdam: 010 Publishers.

28   www.paramo.co.uk/

29   www.keepandshare.co.uk

30   Brezet, H. (1997), Dynamics in ecodesign practice, *UNEP Industry and Environment,* January–June, pp21–24.

31   Ryan, C. (2000), Dematerialising consumption through service substitution is a design challenge, *Industrial Ecology,* 4(1), p5.

32   Euromonitor (2000), *European Marketing Data and Statistics 2000,* 35th Edition, London: Euromonitor.

33   www.interfaceeurope.com/

34   www.sustainablepss.org/casestudies/interface/interface.php

35   Crehan, S. (2005), *Leasing Clothing, a Scenario Analysis*, Cambridge: University of Cambridge, Department of Engineering.

36   Manzini, E. (1994), Design, environment and social quality: From 'existenzminimum' to 'quality maximum', *Design Issues*, 10(1), pp37–43.

Chapter 7

1   Allwood, J. M., Laursen, S. E., Malvido de Rodriguez, C. and Bocken, N. M. P. (2006), *Well Dressed?*, Cambridge: University of Cambridge Institute of Manufacturing, p12.

2   Thorpe, A. (2007), *The Designer's Atlas to Sustainability*, Washington DC: Island Press, pp48–49.

3   Brand, S. (1999), *The Clock of the Long Now*, London: Phoenix.

4   Cooper, T. (1994), *Beyond Recycling: The Longer Life Option*, London: New Economics Foundation.

5   Mackenzie, D. (1997), *Green Design: Design for the Environment*, 2nd edition, London: Laurence King.

6   Paakkunainen, R. (1995), *Textiles and the Environment*, Eindhoven: European Design Centre.

7   Fletcher, K. T. (1999), *Environmental Improvement by Design: An Investigation of the UK Textile Industry*, PhD thesis, London: Chelsea College of Art & Design, The London Institute.

8   Thorpe, A. (2004), Time in design, in E. van Hinte (ed), *Eternally Yours Time in Design: Product Value Sustenance*, Rotterdam: 010 Publishers.

9   www.keepandshare.co.uk/

10   www.barbour.com/

11   Chapman, J. (2005), *Emotionally Durable Design: Objects, Experiences and Empathy*, London: Earthscan.

12   The work of Sigrid Smits is described in E. van Hinte (ed) (1997), *Eternally Yours: Visions on Product Endurance*, Rotterdam: 010 Publishers.

13   van Hinte, E. (ed) (1997), *Eternally Yours: Visions on Product Endurance*, Rotterdam: 010 Publishers.

14   www.kulturservern.se/wronsov/italyanavlusu/italyan_BookletODA-transCS.pdf

15   Franklin Associates (1993), Resource and Environmental Profile Analysis of a Manufactured Apparel Product: Woman's knit polyester blouse, Washington DC: American Fiber Manufacturers Association, ppES–8

16   Thackara, J. (2005), *In the Bubble*, Cambridge, Massachusetts: The MIT Press, p29.

17   Manzini, E. and Jégou, F. (2003), *Sustainable Everyday: Scenarios for Urban Life*, Milan: Edizioni Ambiente, p48.

18   Allwood, J. M., Laursen, S. E., Malvido de Rodriguez, C. and Bocken, N. M. P. (2006), *Well Dressed?*, Cambridge: University of Cambridge Institute of Manufacturing, p4.

19   Adapted from Benyus, J. (1997), *Biomimicry*, New York: Quill, pp252–253

20   The Lifetimes Project was conducted by Kate Fletcher and Mathilda Tham and completed in 2004. It was funded by the Arts and Humanities Research Board. For more information see www.lifetimes.info

Chapter 8

1   *Clone Town Britain*, Report from the New Economics Foundation www.neweconomics.org/gen/news_clonetownbritainresults.aspx

2   von Busch, O. (2005), *The Reform Manual*, available from www.selfpassage.org

3   Illich, I. (1975), *Tools for Conviviality*, London: Fontana.

4   Toffler, A. (1970), *Future Shock*, New York City: Random House.

5   www.bust.com/

6   Stoller, D. (2003), *Stitch 'n Bitch: The Knitters Handbook*, New York: Workman Publishing.

7   Leadbetter, C. and Miller, P. (2004), *The Pro-Am Revolution*, London: Demos.

8   Raunio, A-M. (1995), Favourite clothes – a look at individuals' experience of clothing, in U. Suojanen (ed), *Clothing and Its Social, Psychological, Cultural and Environmental Aspects*, Proceedings of a symposium on textiles, clothing and craft design, Helsinki, 18–20 May, pp179–194.

9   www.alabamachanin.com

10   See for example, Thorpe, A. (2007), *The Designer's Atlas of Sustainability*, Washington DC: Island Press, and Fuad-Luke, A. (2007), Redefining the purpose of (sustainable) design: Enter the design enablers, catalysts in co-design, in J. Chapman and N. Gant (eds), *Designers, Visionaries and Other Stories*, London: Earthscan.

11   von Busch, O. (2005), *Re-forming Appearance: Subversive Strategies in the Fashion System – Reflections on Complementary Modes of Production*, available from www.selfpassage.org

12   Ehrenfeld, J. R. (2004), Searching for sustainability: No quick fix, *Reflections*, 5(8), p7.

13   Speth, James Gustave (2005), *Red Sky at Morning: America and the Crisis of the Global Environment*, New Haven: Yale University.

14   www.infed.org/community/jazz.htm

15   www.mujionline.co.uk/

16   Fuad-Luke, A. (2007), Redefining the purpose of (sustainable) design: Enter the design enablers, catalysts in co-design, in J. Chapman and N. Gant (eds), *Designers, Visionaries and Other Stories*, London: Earthscan, p59.

17   von Busch, O. (2005), *Re-forming Appearance: Subversive Strategies in the Fashion System – Reflections on Complementary Modes of Production*, available from www.selfpassage.org, p10.

18   Gablik, S, (1991), *The Re-enchantment of Art*, London: Thames and Hudson, p62.

19   Thackara, J. (2005), *In the Bubble*, Cambridge, Massachusetts: The MIT Press, p119.

20   http://citizenfashion.com/

21   Walker, S. (2007), Design redux, in J. Chapman and N. Gant (eds), *Designers, Visionaries and Other Stories*, London: Earthscan, p83.

22   Details of the Reform project and von Busch's other work can be found at http://selfpassage.org

23   von Busch, O. (2005), *Re-forming Appearance: Subversive Strategies in the Fashion System – Reflections on Complementary Modes of Production*, available from www.selfpassage.org

24   von Busch, O. (2005), *Re-forming Appearance: Subversive Strategies in the Fashion System – Reflections on Complementary Modes of Production*, available from www.selfpassage.org, p16.

25   www.matrushka.com/

26   www.dosurf.com/

27   www.5ways.info/

Appendix Image Sources

Chapter 1

Eco jeans in 100 per cent organic cotton with sustainable product components and production processes by Levi's
Image courtesy of Levi Strauss

White 100 per cent African cotton dress by Noir
Image courtesy of Noir. Photography: Marc Høm

Ardalanish organic wool tweed by Isle of Mull Weavers
Image courtesy of Ardalanish Isle of Mull Weavers

Bette hemp dress by Enamore
Image courtesy of Enamore. Photography: Richard Bridge

Woven fabric in 100 per cent peace silk by Denise Bird Woven Textiles
Image courtesy of Denise Bird Woven Textiles and Shri Shradhey Ji Maharaj

T-shirt in 100 per cent Ingeo produced as part of the 'Genetic Modification' collection by Moral Fervor, inspired by the quandary surrounding GM technology
Image courtesy of Moral Fervor

Black dress in bamboo viscose by Linda Loudermilk
Image courtesy of Linda Loudermilk

Suit in lyocell by Linda Loudermilk
Image courtesy of Linda Loudermilk

Yarn made from 50 per cent recycled London textiles and 50 per cent pure new wool by EcoAnnie
Image courtesy of Annie Sherburne. Photography: Annie Sherburne

Chapter 2

T-shirts in 100 per cent Fairtrade mark cotton by Marks and Spencer
Image courtesy of M&S

ONE T-shirt made from 100 per cent Lesotho cotton by EDUN
Image courtesy of EDUN

Pillows produced by Armenian craftspeople supported by Aid to Artisans
Image courtesy of Aid to Artisans

Made-By button indicating supply chain transparency
Image courtesy of Made-By

Purple hooded sweatshirt by American Apparel
Image courtesy of American Apparel

Slip dress in 100 per cent silk by Dosa
Image courtesy of Dosa

Chapter 3

Modular garments designed for low laundering
Image by Lucy Jane Batchelor

No Wash top produced as part of the 5 Ways Project
Image courtesy of Kate Fletcher & Becky Earley. Photography: Tom Gidley

Stain dress by Lauren Montgomery Devenney
Image courtesy of Lauren Montgomery Devenney

Chapter 4

Windows blanket by LoooLo
Image courtesy of Joanna Notkin at LoooLo Textiles

back2Back dress by Junky Styling
Image courtesy of Junky Styling. Photography: Ness Sherry

Re-used yarn vest by Muji
Image courtesy of Muji

Synchilla Snap-T fleece by Patagonia made with 85 per cent recycled content, and completely recyclable through the Common Threads Recycling Programme
Image courtesy of Patagonia

Upholstery fabric in wool and ramie by Climatex Lifecycle
Image courtesy of ROHNER Textil AG

Chapter 5

Caress Dress produced as part of the 5 Ways Project
Image courtesy of Kate Fletcher & Becky Earley. Photography: Becky Earley

Organic cotton T-shirt and jeans by Howies
Image courtesy of Howies

Green contrasting stitching on organic cotton T-shirt by American Apparel
Image courtesy of American Apparel

Modular concept top formed by construction of hexagonal fabric pieces that can be removed and replaced when needed or completely deconstructed and rebuilt by Ariel Bishop
Image courtesy of Ariel Bishop. Photography: Nick Schreiner

Chapter 6

Skull dress by Project Alabama
Image courtesy of Alabama Chanin. Photography: Natalie Chanin

Jacket made from 100 per cent hemp grown in England from fibre grown and processed by Bioregional
Image courtesy of Bioregional

Fly skirt in organic tweed, part of the Ardalanish Collection by Anja Hynynen for Isle of Mull Weavers
Image courtesy of Ardalanish Isle of Mull Weavers

Moth blanket by Joanna Notkin
Image courtesy of Joanna Notkin

Efficient pattern cutting concept shirt to address wastage by Andrew Hague. The basic shirt pattern is manipulated to fill the entire fabric, affecting the proportions of the new garment and its design
Image courtesy of Andrew Hague

JP Donleavy shrug, Spring/Summer 2005, 100 per cent cotton by Keep and Share
Image courtesy of Keep and Share. Photography: Meg Hodson

Chapter 7

Eugenia dress, Spring/Summer 2006, 100 per cent cotton by Keep and Share
Image courtesy of Keep and Share. Photography: Meg Hodson

Blue velour pleated furnishing fabric by Sigrid Smits
Fabric courtesy of Sigrid Smits. Photography: Jonathan Moore

Oversized labels and clothes rails in Itaylan Avlusu project swap 'shop' set up by Otto von Busch
Images by Otto von Busch from the Itaylan Avlusu project together with Oda-projesi

One night wonder
Image by Lucy Jane Batchelor

Fancy pants
Image by Lucy Jane Batchelor

Who wears the trousers?
Image by Lucy Jane Batchelor

Great coat
Image by Lucy Jane Batchelor

Chapter 8

Hand-stitched recycled quilt by Alabama Chanin
Image courtesy of Alabama Chanin. Photography: Natalie Chanin

High bag pants by Wronsov a.k.a. Otto von Busch
Image courtesy of Otto von Busch. Photography:conjunction.se

Short sleeve suit, vest suit and oblique collar shirt by Wronsov a.k.a. Otto von Busch
Image courtesy of Otto von Busch. Photography: conjunction.se

T-construction night at Matrushka
Image courtesy of Matrushka

do shirt by do/KesselsKramer (www.dosurf.com)
Image courtesy of do/KesselsKramer. Photography: Maurice Scheltens

Updatable T-shirt produced as part of the 5 Ways Project
Image courtesy of Kate Fletcher & Becky Earley. Photography: Becky Earley

Index

MAR 2 8 2009